C0-AWL-576

The Apostolic Life

M. H. VICAIRE, O. P.

The Apostolic Life

PREFACE

by

Rt. Rev. Msgr. John D. Fitzgerald, J.C.D.

THE PRIORY PRESS, CHICAGO, ILL.

Originally published in French under the title *L'imitation des Apôtres* by Les Éditions du Cerf, Paris, 1963. Translated into English by William E. DeNaple.

Imprimi potest: Gilbert J. Graham, O.P., Provincial. *Nihil obstat*: Thomas C. Donlan, O.P., Bernard O'Riley, O.P., Censores Deputati. *Imprimatur*: Most Rev. Cletus F. O'Donnell, J. C. D., Vicar General, Archdiocese of Chicago, December 22, 1965.

The *Nihil obstat* and *Imprimatur* are official declarations that a book or pamphlet is free of doctrinal or moral error. No implication is contained therein that those who have granted the *Nihil obstat* and *Imprimatur* agree with the contents, opinions, or statements expressed.

Library of Congress Catalogue Number 66-17483

2005 South Ashland Avenue, Chicago, Illinois 60608
Manufactured in the United States of America

Preface

For nearly a century the popes have been laying the groundwork for the age of the lay apostolate. It is no longer a strange idea that the apostolate is in some way the concern of every Christian and is a direct concern of vast numbers of the laity. What the apostolate is needs to be deeply and widely understood. This little book can play an essential role in developing that understanding.

Is it an exaggeration to say an essential role? It is not intended to be. The expression was chosen with care. If the lay apostolate is to be securely rooted in Christian reality it must be a normal, healthy growth in the irreversible pattern of the Church's life. In making sure that it is, history cannot be ignored.

Though in one sense the Church is timeless, nevertheless, as we experience it the Church is a living, historical reality. Its present life and thought can be understood only by those who have profoundly studied and pondered how it came to be what it is now. This Father Vicaire has done in regard to the scripturally-inspired notion of the imitation of the apostles, the apostolic life, the apostolate.

Father Vicaire ranks among the best living medieval historians and is internationally recognized as the foremost authority on St. Dominic and the foundation of the Preaching Friars. His massive and well-nigh definitive *St. Dominic and His Times* (see Bibliography) was published in English translation in 1964. During the many years devoted to research on the foundation of the first religious order devoted to apostolic preaching he became impressed with the evolution of the concept "apostolic"—from the time of the apostles themselves to the time of St. Dominic. With the foundation of the Preachers the various elements of the "apostolic ideal" were fused, and this achievement had to be meticulously thought out. This little book is a carefully-worked historical tracer on a theme always intriguing to Christians.

There has always been a certain tension in Christian life between the demands of the contemplative life and those of the active life. This tension is especially acute during periods of great vitality, such as we are fortunately experiencing during these years of our own lifetime. It is important that we not resolve the tension by more or less eliminating the one or the other. In either case the result is devastating to the true Christian life. The temptation to eliminate the active life is not likely to be a rejection of its importance. The great contemplative saints have always shared the active life of the Church in many ways, but especially by praying for its fruitfulness. St. Therese of the Infant Jesus, for example, is the Patroness of the Missions. The danger today is rather the temptation to minimize the contemplative foundation of any genuine Christian activity. This interesting and significant little historical study should help to overcome that temptation.

Father Vicaire makes the very good point that the history of the Church is a profound commentary on Scripture. How have Christians understood and lived the words of the Scripture in the past? Here he notes the particular texts which gave rise to the notion of the apostolic life, how these texts were understood at various times, and therefore what elements the Church discovers in the true and full imitation of the apostles. It should provide much food for thought to those who sincerely wish to do their part in carrying on the apostolate in the Church today.

Like any living organism the Church is constantly renewing itself. These wonderful days of *aggiornamento* certainly form a period of extraordinary vitality. Such vigorous development can easily produce distortions which must later be painfully excised.

Close touch with history can do much to preserve balance. Those who speak and write about the apostolate and those who are devoted to living it will refine their thinking and increase the fruitfulness of their work by submitting consciously and intelligently to the lessons of history, for "those who ignore history are condemned to live through it again."

John D. Fitzgerald
Ascension Church
Oak Park, Illinois
January 15, 1965

Contents

Bibliography

The historical importance of the theme of the "apostolic life" is widely recognized today. In 1937 Père Vicaire did an essay on this subject (see below), but much has been contributed to its development since. The present book reassesses the question in the light of this work as well as of further research by the author himself.

The works in this Bibliography are cited frequently in the text. For the sake of brevity they are cited merely by the author's name, unless several works by the same author are listed. In the latter case the author's name and the key words of the title are used.

Amand, D., *L'ascèse monastique de S. Basile. Essai historique.* (Mardesous, 1949), pp. 128-29.

Auf der Maur, I., *Mönchtum u. Glaubensverkündigung in den Schriften des Hl. Johannes Chrysostomus* (Fribourg, 1959), pp. 75, 143, notes 10, 11; 147 and notes 5-10; 174 and notes 3,4.

Bacht, H., "Heimweh nach der Urkirche, Zur Wesensdeutung des frühchristlichen Mönchtums," *Liturgie u. Mönchtum,* 7 (1950), 64-78.

Dereine, Ch., "Vie commune, règle de S. Augustin et chanoines réguliers au XIe siècle," *Revue d'histoire ecclésiastique,* 41 (1946), 365-406.

———, "Le problème de la vie commune chez les canonistes, d'Anselme de Lucques à Gratien," *Studi Gregoriani,* 3 (1948), 287-98.

———, "Chanoines," in *Dictionnaire d'histoire et de géographie ecclésiastiques,* XII:353-405, especially 377.

———, *Les chanoines réguliers au diocèse de Liège avant saint Norbert* (Brussels, 1952), pp. 15-32.

Dickinson, J.C., *The Origins of the Austin Canons and Their Introduction into England* (London, 1950), pp. 52-58.

Leclercq, J., *La vie parfaite* (Paris, 1948), pp. 82-105.

Morin, G., *L'idéal monastique et la vie chrétienne des premiers jours* (5th ed.; Paris, 1931), pp. 66-68.

Moureaux, A., "La vie apostolique, à propos de Rupert de Deutz," *Revue lit. et monast.,* 21 (1936), 71-78, 125-41, 264-76.

Olphe-Galliard, M., "Cassien," in *Dictionnaire de Spiritualité,* II:232.

Siegwart, J., *Die Chorherren u. Chorfrauengemeinschaften in der deutschsprachigen Schweiz vom 6. Jahrh. bis 1160* (Fribourg, 1962), pp. 231-56.

Spaetling, L., *De apostolicis, pseudo-apostolis, apostolinis* (Munich, 1947), pp. 20-24, 43-110.

Vicaire, M.-H. "The Rule of St. Augustine, Teacher of the Apostolic Life," in P. Mandonnet, *St. Dominic and His Work,* trans. M.B. Larkin (St. Louis and London, 1944), pp. 258-90.

———, *St. Dominic and His Times,* trans. K. Pond (New York, Toronto, London, 1964), pp. 37-39, 72-76, 89, 173-75, 311, 315-17.

Introduction

THE APOSTLE

Representations of the apostles often appear on the ancient monuments of Christianity: the mosaics of Ravenna or of Rome, Roman frescoes and cornices, the arches of Gothic portals, fifteenth-century choir stalls—where they alternate with the representations of the prophets—the miniatures in medieval Books of Hours. They are pictured as ascetics in long robes with bare feet, their faces severe and surmounted by halos. Sometimes they surround and listen to Christ; sometimes they bear witness to the Messiah by the holy book which they clutch against their breast or by the particular instrument of their martyrdom. Although they are represented individually at times, more often they appear as a group, assembled for the washing of the feet or gathered together devoutly at the Last Supper. Other times they are shown in a moment of inspiration, confirmed by the apparition of the Risen Christ with his wounds, inflamed by the mission which they are receiving from Christ—as on the spandrel of the narthex of Vezelay—illuminated by the grace of Pentecost.

Do these lofty figures still convey to Christians the fullness of the message which they were charged to preach? Certainly we continue to see in them a memorial to the life of Christ, an illustration of the Gospel, the commemoration of the foundation of the Church, the invocation of powerful protectors whose names are freely given at baptism: Peter, Paul, James, John, Philip, etc. However, the principal lesson that Christians of earlier times learned from the representation of the apostles was something quite other. The image of the apostles was for them a book in which they were eager to discover the art of the perfect life. For, in their eyes, the apostles were the models of the full Christian spirit, its living norms. Their figures helped to recall its complete formulation even to details.

Were not these apostles intimately associated in the life and death of Christ in order later to be his witnesses even to the ends of the earth? And what an intimate association! "No longer do I call you servants . . . but I have called you friends, for all that I have heard from my Father I have made known to you" (Jn. 15:15). Had they not been formed slowly by Jesus himself, in the rhythm of his divine, progressive, applied pedagogy? For example, when Jesus sent them, two-by-two, to preach, he minutely described for them the way to behave in announcing the kingdom of God. It is as if he wished to accustom them, by repeated trials, to the manner in which they should speak and act after his Resurrection. He formed them into models that they might be "examples to the flock" (1 Pt. 5:3; 2 Thes. 3:9). Whence the unabashed expression of St. Paul: "Be imitators of me, as I am of Christ" (1 Cor. 11:1; 4:16). Imitate the apostles? Of course! Both in their persons and by their institutions they were the formulators of the original Christian archetype in the church of Jerusalem. That is why their descendants created memory-prodding images of them.

The familiarity of the image, joined to reflection on the sacred writings, contributed to popularizing the idea that the *vita* or *conversatio apostolica,* as the texts say, was the model of the perfect life. Thus, at every step of the movement of perfection in the Church, whether in its beginnings or in its renewals, this idea appears among the reformers as a leitmotiv, the intention of observing in its fullness some forgotten or unrecognized element of the "way of life of the apostles." From Egyptian ascetics to contemporary communities of parish priests, unnumbered hermits, canons, itinerant preachers, mendicant religious, missionaries, and diocesan priests propose to rediscover this way of life at its source, in the hope of better answering to the call of God.

Surprisingly enough, the direct heirs of the apostolic ministry, the clergy, were not the ones who gave the impetus to this movement; rather, the ascetics, the anchorites, and the cenobites, were the first born of the movement toward perfection in the Church. It is particularly interesting, then, to examine how the great heralds of the monastic movement, in instituting, developing, reforming a way of life which gave promise of a fruitful future, explicitly proposed to reproduce a way of life such as Jesus had wished. It was a way of life which the apostles had accepted and delineated by their lives as well as by their words and of which a number of texts of the New Testament still pass the message on to us today.

1

The Monks

1. THE APOSTOLIC MODEL OF THE CHRISTIAN

Among the texts of the New Testament which in the eyes of the monks were the apostolic sources of their ideal, the most important were the phrases of the Gospel which settled upon one or another of the apostles a command to follow. Among all these words of personal commands, none are more important than the calls, the "vocations." The monks considered the famous "Come follow me" of Jesus to be the beginning of the *conversatio apostolica* of the Twelve. But it can be the same for others; it was not addressed only to the apostles. The rich young man also heard it: "If you would be perfect, go, sell what you possess and give to the poor, and you will have treasure in heaven; and come, follow me" (Mt. 19:21). To this vocation the monks, imitating those of apostolic times, also answered yes.

The Gospel also contains counsels or precepts addressed to the Twelve as a group. The accounts of the preaching mission of the apostles yield a good number of them, which will be pointed out when the canons and especially the mendicant religious are discussed. Nevertheless even the monks would occasionally seize upon them.

In the letters of St. Paul a number of phrases of the same type can be found. The apostle par excellence recommends certain attitudes or customs to which he was strongly attached. The monks paid special attention to what he had to say about manual labor. Paul's purpose was to be independent, to owe nothing to any man. The monks saw here a fundamental element of the *vita apostolica* as they claimed to live it.

However, in all the New Testament, what impressed the monks most were the descriptions of the primitive common life found in the Acts of the Apostles. The first chapters of this book contain four passages which the exegetes designate as "summaries," groups of parallel verses which describe the same series of attitudes in repeated strokes. The two principal ones, which are re-echoed throughout this story of the early Christians, are these: "Now the company of those who believed were of one heart and soul, and no one said that any of the things which he possessed was his own, but they had everything in common. And with great power the apostles gave their testimony to the resurrection of the Lord Jesus, and great grace was upon them all. There was not a needy person among them, for as many as were possessors of lands or houses sold them, and brought the proceeds of what was sold and laid it at the apostles' feet; and distribution was made to each as any had need" (Acts 4:32-35). The second text is almost the same: "And they devoted themselves to the apostles' teaching and fellowship, to the breaking of bread and the prayers. And fear came upon every soul; and many wonders and signs were done through the apostles. And all who believed were together and had all things in common; and they sold their possessions and goods and distributed them to all, as any had need. And day by day, attending the temple together and breaking bread in their homes, they partook of food with glad and generous hearts, praising God and having favor with all the people. And the Lord added to their number day-by-day those who were being saved" (Acts 2:42-47).

These verses are the precious jewels of the first chapters of the Acts. In them we are still able to hear echoes of the Church's origins. For good reason, then, exegetes assign them the highest importance. The monks also noticed them, examined them, and lovingly scrutinized them. For many centuries they considered these verses the special source of their ideal. Numerous texts on this point, dating from the origins of monasticism to its magnificent flowering in the twelfth century with the Cistercians, could be cited. Texts from Citeaux could be mentioned, but the attitude of Cluny at this time was the same. Evidence of this is found in a beautiful passage written by Clunisian Abbot William of Saint-Thierry (near Reims), who was later to be a disciple of St. Bernard. About 1122 he describes the history of the monastic life in this manner: "But we come to this spiritual society of which the apostle Paul spoke to the Philippians[1] in praise of the regular discipline and of the sublime joy of brothers living together in unanimity. To do justice to this discipline it is necessary to return to its beginning in the time of the apostles. Since it was the apostles themselves who instituted it as their own way of life, according to the teaching of the Lord, unless it was the grace of the Holy Spirit which gave them power from above to live together in such a way that all would have but one heart and one soul, so that everything would be held in common, so that all would be continually in the temple in a spirit of harmony. Animated by a great love for this form of life instituted by the apostles, certain men wished no longer to have any other house or any other lodging than the house of God, the house of prayer. All that they did they did according to a common pro-

[1] 2:1-5 (unanimity, imitation of Christ); 3:17 (imitation of Paul).

gram, under a common rule; in the name of the Lord they lived together, possessing nothing of their own, not even their bodily strength, nor were they even masters of their own will. They lay down to sleep at the same time, they rose up together, they prayed, they sang psalms, they studied together. They showed the fixed and changeless will of being obedient to their superiors and of being entirely submissive to them. They kept their needs to a minimum and lived with very little; they had poor clothes, a mean diet, and limited everything according to a very precise rule."[2]

This text leaves no doubt. The monks of the twelfth century genuinely considered that they were continuing the common life preached and practiced by the apostles. But this idea flourished for eight centuries, and the affirmation, frequently renewed, of the apostolic origins of the monastic state is no vague allusion. It is a precise declaration, a reasoned conviction, resting, from the fourth century, in the eyes of its authors on two facts that they believed completely established. One was the Egyptian origin of monasticism, which no one would question. The other, and this one is quite questionable, is that the Egyptian Christians lived a way of life identical to that of Jerusalem.

[2]*Liber de natura et dignitate amoris*, chap. 9, *PL* 184: 395B-396D. Written in 1122 in the Abbey of Saint-Thierry.

Eusebius of Caesarea, in his history of the Church from the beginnings to the fourth century (303-325), is responsible for the second affirmation.[3] He was under the impression that he had discovered in the writings of Philo of Alexandria proof that the customs of life taught by the apostles to the church of Jerusalem were extended likewise to Alexandria in Egypt and even farther. In his work on the contemplative life, which dates before the year 40, Philo described a very curious institution whose inhabitants he called the "Therapeutae." These men lived in the desert, followed an edifying common life, practiced strict poverty, held everything in common, and distributed to each according to his needs. During the period of their common life they read the books of the ancients and practiced very extended fasts, some even resolving to eat only once every three days and some only once in six days. Finally, the room in which they prayed, still following Philo, was called the *monasterion.*

Eusebius was very impressed. The Therapeutae lived exactly as the first Christians did according to the Acts of the Apostles: they practiced poverty, holding everything in common, distributing to each

[3]Bk. II, chap. 17, ed. by Bardy (Paris, 1952), pp. 72-77. The various passages of the *De vita contemplativa* which Eusebius sums up and comments upon are to be found in the edition of Conybeare (Oxford, 1895), pp. 26-123.

according to his needs. The ancient books which they read must have been the apostolic writings, such as the Epistle to the Hebrews and the letters of Paul, and of course the Gospels. Their fasts are doubtless those of the first Christians. Eusebius ends his long and minute analysis: "That Philo wrote all of this, thinking of the first heralds of the evangelical teaching and of the usages transmitted from the beginnings by the apostles, is evident to all." Thus the apostolic life of the church in Jerusalem was extended to Africa in the time of Philo. In considering more closely the witness of Philo it becomes evident that this kind of life was instituted not only at Alexandria itself, but much farther, beyond Lake Mareotis and even in many other countries of the world. Eusebius concluded that the form of the primitive life described by the Acts of the Apostles was not established at Jerusalem alone, nor even only in Judea, but that it was far more widespread, that it reached Egypt in the time of St. Mark, and finally that it took root in other countries, probably those in which St. Paul preached. Thus a life of prayer and poverty, harmonious and communal, had existed everywhere in the primitive Church.

Eusebius did not draw his idea of this life from the life of the monks, although he did use the words "apostolic ascetics" and even "monastery."[4] Monasticism properly so-called did not yet exist. But a half century later the connection would be perfectly clear. St. Jerome, in chapters eight and eleven of his *De viris illustribus* (392), seized upon the information of Eusebius and of Philo on the Therapeutae and concluded: "It is evident that the Church of the first believers in Christ was indeed such as the monks now desire and strive to be. That nothing should be held as one's own; that there should be neither rich nor poor among them; that whatever they brought with them should be shared among those who were in need; that they should give themselves to prayer and to psalms, as well as to study and to continence. Is this not how Luke portrays the believers of Jerusalem?"[5]

Cassian, some thirty years later—he wrote between 419 and 428—did not satisfy himself merely with comparing, he claimed a definite continuity. Rereading what Eusebius had written on the origins of the church of Alexandria and on the Therapeutae, he specifies that the monks received this way of life from St. Mark, and even that they have improved upon the practices imposed by the apostles on the church of Jerusalem, or rather on the entire primi-

[4] *Ibid.*, pp. 72,74. On the theme of apostolic asceticism in Origen and in Eusebius, *cf.* Spaetling, pp. 21 f.
[5] *PL* 23:654-658.

tive Church.[6] He established then the theory that would become classical and that would be found, as if by custom and often reduced to a schema, even in the bulls of the medieval popes.

From the beginning the apostles had established a communal life or apostolic life as described in the Acts for everyone in the Church. This life was extended to the whole body of the faithful including the church of Alexandria. St. Paul, however, introduced a completely disconcerting element. He taught that upon the Gentiles, who unlike the Alexandrian Jews had not been prepared to assume the rigors of the primitive life, should be imposed only the four ritual precepts of which the famous gathering called the Council of Jerusalem had spoken (Acts 15:5-29). The hierarchy, however, finally thought it fitting for all the faithful to be held only to the kind of life to which the Gentile converts had been bound. Therefore it was no longer necessary to renounce everything as was done in the beginning. In this way a form of life became common in the Church which was inferior to the way of life of the primitive Church and which put an end to the communal life. Some were not agreeable to it. The monks clung to the more perfect kind of life. Continuing the tradition of the church of Jerusalem

[6]See *Institutiones coenobiorum,* Bk. II, chap. 5, *PL* 49: 84-88. Written between 419-426.

established by the apostles, they set up definite communities, isolated from the rest of the Church, in which they preserved as a precious thing the vitality of primitive Christianity. This is what the Abbot Piammon discusses in the eighteenth conference of the *Collationum XXIV collectio,* where Cassian gives an account of conferences with some of the principal ascetics or monks of the desert.[7] And here is the conclusion of the conference: "But those who still live in the apostolic fervor [The expression "apostolic fervor" is well used! It evokes the tongues of fire which descended upon the apostles on Pentecost.] preserve the memory of this primitive perfection by going far away from their cities and from the company of those who consider illicit for themselves and for the Church of God the negligence of an easy life. Thus they went to live in the woods or in obscure places and strove to practice, privately and as if it were a particular law, the rules instituted by the apostles for the whole body of the Church. This discipline of life of which we speak is not lost among the disciples of those who separated themselves from these contagions. These men who isolated themselves from the crowd of the faithful were later called monks or 'lonely ones,' because they abstained from mar-

[7]Collatio XVIII, *PL* 49:1094B-1100A. Written between 426-428. Cf. Olephe-Galliard, col. 232.

riage and separated themselves from their families and from the world by the severe practice of the solitary life. They are justly called cenobites, since they drew together in the community of life."

Cassian is one of the authors most appreciated in the convents. Constantly reread by novices and monks, his conferences fashioned the medieval monastic life—and even the modern monastic life. Such a reading of history could not be sterile. The conviction of Cassian would influence subsequent monks and would play a large part in turning more than ever the eyes of those who wished to give themselves to the life of Christian perfection toward the origins of the Church, toward the great model of the apostles and of the community of the cenacle.

At the beginning of the thirteenth century Conrad of Clairvaux gathered together the Cistercian compilation that is called the *Great Exordium.* The prologue he gave it is a history of the monastic life down to the least detail, inspired by the text of Cassian.[8] Similarly inspired in the first quarter of the preceding century was the polemicist who defended the monks against the canons and the secular clerics in the little work called *De vita vere*

[8]See *Exordium Magnum cisterciense,* chaps. 2, 3, *PL* 185:997-999.

apostolica.[9] This vision was therefore a general one. When a William of Saint-Thierry, a St. Bernard,[10] even an Abelard,[11] represented their monastic life as an apostolic life, they intended to signify, just as did the monk of the fifth century, that they were continuing the exalted life prescribed by the apostles to the infant Church and practiced by them. Since many Christians, yielding to the temptation to a lower form of life infinitely less conformed to the inspiration of the Spirit who breathed upon the first faithful, had later abandoned this apostolic life, what was the value of this conviction? Was it authentic? Did it truly correspond to reality and to the intentions of the founders of the monastic life?

2. NOSTALGIA FOR THE EARLY CHURCH

The yearning to live as the early Christians did grew out of an error of fact, namely, a false gen-

[9]Chap. 4, *PL* 170:643-653. Martène attributes this opuscule, not without reasons, to Rupert of Tuy (Deutz); Dereine thinks it the work of Honorius of Autun; others of a monk of Brunwylers near the Abbey of Tuy. None are completely convincing.

[10]"Ordo noster qui primus fuit in Ecclesia, imo a quo coepit Ecclesia . . . cujus Apostoli institutores . . . inchoatores extiterunt," *Apologia ad Guillelmum Sti. Theodorici,* chaps. 10, 24, *PL* 182:912BC. On the content of the *Vita apostolica: Sermones de diversis,* 22,2; 27,3; 37,7; *In Cantica Sermo,* 85,12, *PL* 183:515D, 613C, 642CD, 1193D.

[11]*Historia calamitatum,* chap. 7, *PL* 178:131D; *Theologia,* Bk. II, *PL* 178:1179B and especially 1180BC.

eralization of the life of Jerusalem. Eusebius made a mistake when he saw the life of the early Church in the account of the life of the Therapeutae. The Therapeutae, if they had any other existence than in the generous and utopian imagination of Philo, were probably pious ascetics of Jewish origin, lovers of philosophy, who were doubtless few in number and left no trace at all other than the account found in Eusebius. They seem to have been one of those numerous institutions created by the Jewish spirit in the full ardor of its faith. An example of this type of institution is the semimonks of Qumran, the remains of which are being exhumed along the coast of the Dead Sea and which would have remained almost totally unknown to us had not their library been accidently discovered. The Therapeutae are very interesting since they showed the creative ardor of a segment of the Jewish faith at the time of our Lord and the religious purity of this faith. However, they are not able to provide a basis for monastic history, especially as they are represented to us by Eusebius. They were not the first Christians, nor were they the first Christian monks; they were pure Jews of a very religious bent.

Note that, regardless of the error on which Eusebius and Cassian rest a good part of their theories and which therefore somewhat confuses the historical tradition, it is indeed exact that monasticism was inspired from its beginning—not exclusively, but truly—by a desire to imitate the apostles and the first Christians.

Certainly there are elements in monasticism which are not specifically Christian but common to every effort for interior perfection. This general basis of human spirituality explains the existence of real analogies between the monastic institution and institutions far distant from it both in time and in space. On the other hand, the Egyptian beginnings of monasticism resulted in the institution inheriting a certain number of local traditions. The better Orientalists, for example Lefort, have shown that many of the secondary traits of monasticism can be explained by its Egyptian origins better than by Greek or Pythagorian origins. Finally, among the Christian inspirations of monasticism everything cannot be reduced to the imitation of the apostles. Certain biblical themes such as "the angelic life," "prophetic hope," "the royal road," "abnegation," "martyrdom,"[12] have furnished to the monks who meditated on their institution elements of great fruitfulness. Nevertheless the most fundamental Christian factor which historians have discovered in the origins of monasticism is a powerful "nostalgia for the early Church."[13] The principal expres-

[12]Leclercq, p. 170; Bacht, p. 66; Auf der Maur, p. 174 give us a certain number of these themes.

[13]This is the general theme of Bacht in the article cited.

sion of this was the wish to take up the "apostolic life," that is to say, the Christian mentality communicated by the apostles to the early Church and lived by them. This is not surprising if it is remembered that the early monks were convinced of the universality of the formula of the Christian life described in the Acts as pertaining to Jerusalem.

At the heart of monasticism and indeed the very stuff out of which it was created is the anchoritism of the hermits: the flight to the desert and the solitary life. The eremitical life down through the centuries was the primitive nebula from which, as stars, the institutions or movements of perfection in the Church were shaped. It can be said that in every true religious there is something of the hermit, an element often almost totally ignored, but an inclination which is always there. The eremitical life, the origin of the monastic movement, was inspired expressly by the appeal to total renunciation addressed by Christ to the apostles and through them to all of the first Christians (Mt. 19:21). The account by St. Athanasius of the conversion of St. Anthony, one of the most ancient documents concerning the eremitical and monastic life, is significant of the whole tradition.

"One day as Anthony reflected upon why the apostles had abandoned everything at the call of Jesus to follow him and the first Christians had sold their goods to place them at the feet of the apostles for distribution to the poor, and on the wonderful hope such people would have in heaven, he entered the basilica and heard in the gospel which was being read at that very moment the account of the call of the young man: 'If you would be perfect, go, sell what you have and give to the poor, and come follow me, and you shall have treasure in heaven.'" He, himself, then sold what he had and went to the desert.[14]

As these flights to the desert became more and more common, various types of eremitical associations among the solitaries began to be organized in Egypt. In time the common life made its appearance. The powerful but unstable influence of the eremitical life then passed into an institution which gave it form and equilibrium and rendered it fruitful. This was the cenobitic life of Pachomius (about 320). But when one has recourse to the texts relevant to the substantial fortunate transformation of the flight into the desert into the community life, one again encounters the significance of the documents concerning the life of the apostles.[15]

The most ancient lives of St. Pachomius, written in the Coptic language, attribute to the founder the

[14]*Vita Antonii*, chap. 2, *PG* 26:842-846.

[15]K. Heussi (*Der Ursprung des Mönchtums*, Tübingen, 1936), having expressly denied it, Th. Lefort vigorously reasserted it in *Rev. d'hist. ecclésiastique*, 33 (1937), 345 f.

explicit intention of renewing the perfect community "according to what is written concerning the believers in the Acts of the Apostles."[16] The coadjutor and successor of the Saint, Horsiisi, made identical protestations according to the book that is known as his testament.[17] The second successor, but direct disciple of the founder, Theodore of Tabennesi, claimed even to have heard St. Anthony, to whom he went to announce the death of his master, declare that the cenobitic institution of Pachomius surpassed his own and that the grouping of monks into a community realized truly the "apostolic way"; to such an extent that if he were not himself so aged, he would himself take up this way of the apostles.[18] Thus Theodore could declare: "[It is by a favor] of God . . . that the holy *koinonia* appeared [on the earth]; by [that] he made the apostolic life known to men who desire to be images of the apostles before the Lord of all forever. The apostles in effect abandoned everything and with their whole heart followed Christ . . . . After that they deserved to be seated on the twelve thrones

[16]It is a question of the first Sahidic fragment, in Th. Lefort, *Les vies coptes de S. Pachôme et des ses premiers successeurs* (Louvain, 1943), p. 3. *Cf.* pp. 186, 268, 269, 323.

[17]"Liber Horseisius," ed. by A. Boon, in *Pachomiana latina* (Louvain, 1932), 142, n. 40, where Acts 4:32 f. is cited.

[18]Lefort, *Les vies coptes* . . . , pp. 268 f.

of glory and to [judge] the twelve [tribes] of Israel."[19]

The connection between the apostolic Church and the cenobitic life is more clearly, and above all more abundantly, expressed by Theodore, to whom we perhaps owe the stereotyped formula, "apostolic life."[20] Certainly it is fitting for a disciple to set down in formulas and in theories the insights of his master. But to prove that in doing this Theodore did not fundamentally modify the position of St. Pachomius, it is enough to note with the historians[21] the primordial role that the direct inspiration of Holy Scripture or, to speak as Gennadius, his "apostolic grace"[22] held in the work of the founder. At the same time it should be remembered that, at the very period of this foundation, Eusebius

[19]"2e Catéchèse de Théodore," in Th. Lefort, *Oeuvres de S. Pachôme et ses disciples, Scriptores coptici,* 24 (Louvain, 1956), p. 38. Cf. p. 41.

[20]It is this which Siegwart justly emphasizes, p. 237. Nevertheless, to suspect that Theodore is the first to have formulated the theme of the apostolic life, or even to have projected his distinct idea on the documents of his predecessors is not enough to prove that, in doing this, he essentially distorted them.

[21]See H. Bacht, "Antonius u. Pachomius, von der Anachorese zum Cönobitentum," *Studia Anselmiana,* 38 (1956), 92-97.

[22]"Vir tam in docendo quam in signa faciendo apostolicae gratiae," in *De viris illustribus,* chap. 7, ed. by Cushing and Richardson (Leipzig, 1896), p. 63. If the rule of Pachomius did not contain biblical citations, this results from his mode of expression rather than from his mentality.

spread the idea that in Egypt, Rome, and Antioch, the first Christians following the apostles had universally undertaken a life of holy community, similar to that of Jerusalem. The theme of the invitation of the apostles no longer suggested only sensational gestures of abandoning riches and fleeing the world, as it did in the time of St. Anthony and the first anchorites; rather it provided a complete program of the perfect life, a life in community.

Such then, in its beginning, was the apostolic ideal of the movement of the perfect life in the Church. It is of little importance that this movement did not have the historic continuity of passing to monasticism from the life of the early Church. It is not even important that the summaries of the Acts schematized to excess and risked giving a deformed picture of the life of the primitive Church as a result of a somewhat too heavyhanded exegesis. What is essential to our eyes for the moment is the notion that this scriptural schema, such as it was understood by each century in turn, has directly influenced the history of the life of perfection and especially the cenobitic life. This partially justifies Cassian. It is true that he was mistaken and betrayed tradition according to the historical facts. But it was not precisely history which concerned him. His purpose was to affirm the spiritual filiation of the ideal which flourished in his times in the monasteries to that which reigned in the apostolic church of Jerusalem—as he understood it from the text of the Acts. From this point of view he was right.

The expressions then employed to indicate the connections of the monastic movement with the apostles, with the first monks, and with the great founders of the monastic rules are characteristic.[23] The apostles are called "authors of the monastic life," "institutors," "initiators." They were considered responsible for monasticism since they had given it its stamp of authentic and original Christian life. Moreover, they were considered the original models because they were the first to teach and to practice the formulas and the fundamental institutions of the monastic life. To St. Paul the Hermit, to St. Anthony, the title of "founders" is given, because they initiated the monastic life; yet they are called also "conservators," because by the institution of the monasteries, they prevented this spirit, the life of the apostolic Church, from disappearing totally from the world. As for St. Benedict and St. Augustine, authors of the traditional rules, they are called "particular masters" of the monastic life.

[23]Texts cited by Leclercq, pp. 87 f.

3. THE APOSTOLIC OBSERVANCE OF THE MONK

Having established the original "apostolic" inspiration of the monastic movement, it is possible now to enter into details and to explore the attitudes, the practices, the institutions which—in the course of the long history of monasticism—the masters of the monastic life have discovered in the apostolic example. Among these the monastic profession holds the first place. Their reading of the Gospel persuaded the monks that their profession, that is to say their monastic commitment, was prefigured by the commitment of the apostles. They specify even the instant at which this was done. It was in the course of the famous proclamation of St. Peter to the Lord: "Lo, we have left everything and followed you."[24] The common opinion of the monastic masters held that, at that instant, St. Peter made profession in the name of all the apostles. For this reason he went on to add: "What then shall we have?" It was a profession somewhat selfish but precise. Throughout the vast monastic literature it is customary to refer to this act as the "apostolic profession." Thus St. Bernard did not hesitate to designate the monastic profession, or rather the pre-profession which

[24] 19:27. Cf. Leclercq, p. 96 and notes 6 and 51.

was called "the renunciation of the world," *apostolica professio.*[25]

The monks considered that the apostles had also left them an example of a novitiate. Our Lord himself was the Master of novices. Here is a delightful passage from Peter of Celles: "To the religious who were the twelve apostles and the seventy-two disciples Jesus taught the discipline of the cloister; . . . so great was their reverence toward their Master and so great their obedience and their submission, so great their fraternal affection, that never was a breath of discord raised among them, except perhaps when they had a discussion among them to know which held the greater rank, or when they became indignant on the subject of the two brothers who asked to sit the one at the right and the other at the left hand of Jesus. But all the human frailty contained in such fragile vessels not yet sufficiently baked in the fire of the Holy Spirit the hand of the potter reshaped in correcting them. . . . They never wished to be separated from him, and when he announced to them that he was going into Judea, Thomas said to the disciples: 'Let us go with him, that we also might die with him.' "[26]

[25]St. Bernard, *Sermones de diversis,* Sermo 37,7, *PL* 183:642CD; Sermo 27,3, *PL* 183:613C; In Cantica Sermo 85,12, *PL* 183:1193D.

[26]*De disciplina claustrali,* chap. 2, *PL* 202:1101D-1102C.

Like the life of the apostles, the monk's life had for its purpose the perfect practice of the life of charity, which is the beginning and the end of the entire Christian life. This above all Jesus accomplished by the *vita apostolica,* namely, the possibility of living more completely "at the very wellsprings." On this point it is important to consider the words of St. Bernard: "It is your life which makes the apostolic life present to the Church today. What does that mean? The apostles left everything and, gathered together close to the Lord, lived under his tutelage. From the fountain of the Lord they were able to draw the waters of joy, and at the very wellspring itself they drank the water of life. How fortunate the eyes of those who have seen him! But you yourself is it not very much like that for you, even though you no longer live in his presence since he is bodily absent, and you do not hear words from his mouth but from those whom he has sent? Pass on this treasure of having believed on the hearing and the faith of those sent, just as the apostles believed at sight and on the words themselves. Persevere in this state, and just as the apostles kept to the royal road of justice in hunger and thirst, in cold and nakedness, in many laborings, fasts, vigils, and other observances, strive to equal them, not in their merits but in their practices."[27]

The apostles gave the monks the example of a life in the élan of the Spirit, completely animated by the "apostolic fervor" which they received on Pentecost and by which they passed on the secret of receiving and radiating grace. The text of the Acts of the Apostles, immediately after mentioning the communal life, adds, "and great grace was upon them all" (Acts 4:33). This grace manifested itself even by miracles: "And many wonders and signs were done through the apostles" (Acts 2:43). In this way a true monk, who lives in community, possesses an extraordinary grace for radiating sanctity and thus of spreading the Church abroad. He can obtain the power of a miracle worker. The biographers of the great monks and of holy founders sought to emphasize the fact that, because of their great holiness, these men, like the apostles, had received the power of working miracles. Examples are to be found in Cassian's account of the Abbot Abraham,[28] Gennadius' account of St. Pachomius,[29] or St. Gregory's account of St. Benedict.[30]

[27]St. Bernard, Sermo 22,2, *PL* 183:595D-596A.
[28]Coll. 15, chap. 6, *PL* 49:1003A; cf. chap. 1, 990A.
[29]Cf. *supra*, p. 26, n. 4.
[30]*Dialog.*, Bk. II, chap. 32, *PL* 66:188C; cf. chap. 7, 146AB.

The monks also drew from the apostles the example of communal prayer: "And day by day, attending the temple together" (Acts 2:46). Is this not the origin of their liturgical office? Following the apostles and the primitive community, the Church has formed the custom of common recitations at fixed hours which form its official prayer. The apostles clung to this as an essential part of their ministry. Their institution of the diaconate was, as the apostles themselves declared, to "devote ourselves to prayer and to the ministry of the word" (Acts 4:4). The monks took their cue from the apostles: regular prayer to fulfill the precept of the Lord, "that they ought always to pray" (Lk. 18:1; 1 Thes. 5:17). Here we find the origin of the major monastic prayer.

From another point of view it is evident that the monks drew from the apostolic life the fullness of a fraternal community by holding everything in common. With regard to the ordinary necessities of life they had a common table and a common shelter. Their spiritual life was formed around common prayer and the *lectio divina.* With regard to practical activity they engaged in bodily labor and the service of their neighbor. The common development of the moral life was rooted in fraternal correction according to the precepts of the Gospel. From this sprang a variety of institutions of which the chapter of faults is one of the most fruitful. Finally, the entire group was to be dominated by a fraternal spirit: "They wished to have but one heart and one spirit." This unanimity, the earthly fulfillment of fraternal charity as sketched in the fine touch of St. John the evangelist, plays the role of end or purpose in monastic life. Everything else is a means. The developments of the notion of unanimity that can be read in the spiritual writings and in the legislation of the monks are a direct echo of the Acts of the Apostles.

Would it not be entirely fitting that the charity which dominates the interior life of a community of monks should break out to illumine the exterior world in a ministry of salvation? If there is truly an Eastern tradition of monasticism, of which St. Jerome occasionally made himself the defender in the West[31] and which rejects missionary activity for the monks, there is another tradition of which St. John Chrysostom,[32] the Syrian monks, and the Western monastery of Lerins[33] are the most ancient witnesses. This other tradition resolutely turns the

[31]See *Epistula* L, *ad Domnionem*, 4, *PL* 22:514; *Contra Vigilantium Liber*, *PL* 23:367A, reproduced in Gratian, chap. 3, XVI, q. 1. It is the famous text: "Monachus non doctoris sed plangentis habet officium, qui vel se, vel mundum lugeat et Domini pavidus praestoletur adventum." Jerome did not always follow his own advice. See Auf der Maur, 117, n. 3.

[32]See Auf der Maur, pp. 110-14, 130-34, 177-82.

[33]See *ibid.*, pp. 11, 178.

monks toward the evangelization of the pagans, for who is more suited to the preaching of salvation than "men animated by the burning zeal of the apostolic philosophy [by which is meant the life of total renunciation]."[34] These words of John Chrysostom can be annotated by those of St. Nilus (d. 430), his disciple: "A holy life without preaching is more useful than preaching without a holy life. But when a holy life and preaching are joined together, then one achieves the perfect image of the apostolic philosophy!"[35] Obviously the ministry of salvation is included in the imitation of the apostles; this element is so important today that it is the only one to be clearly expressed by the adjective "apostolic,"[36] (from which the noun "apostolate" derives) in modern languages. It is certain, however, that such was not the case during the first twelve centuries of the Church. For St. John Chrysostom[37] himself,

[34]In this way he described the monks he requested of Leontius of Ancyra to evangelize the Goths, according to Theodoret, *Hist. Eccl.*, 5,31, ed. of Parmentier, pp. 330 f. Cf. Auf der Maur, pp. 130 f. On the use of philosophy to signify a type of the perfect life, *ibid.*, pp. 87-92, 130 f., 169 f., and E.T. Bettencourt, "L'idéal religieux de S. Antoine," *Studia Anselmiana*, 38 (1956), 46 and n. 3.

[35]*Epist.*, Bk. III, 243, *PG* 79:496D; cf. *Ep.*, Bk. II, 103, *PG* 79:245BC.

[36]L.M. Dewailly, "Note sur l'histoire de l'adjectif: Apostolique," *Mélanges de science religieuse*, 5 (1946), 141-52.

[37]See Auf der Maur, p. 143, nn. 10,11. But this attitude of life, for St. John Chrysostom, included evangelization, p. 147, n. 5.

as for all ancient tradition, the term "apostolic" is applied essentially to the discipline of life as it was observed by the apostles and by the faithful instructed by the apostles in the early Church, the models of the perfect Christian.

It is, then, from the descriptions of the church of Jerusalem that the monks drew the fundamental discipline of their common life, apostolic poverty. But apostolic poverty was not a total absence of the means of existence, for the community itself had possessions; rather it was a renunciation of personal ownership. This epitomized, in the eyes of the monks, the rule of the apostles. As late as the eleventh century the council of Nimes (1906) stated: "For the monks live according to the rule of the apostles and follow their footsteps in practicing the common life, according as it is written in the Acts of the Apostles: they had but one heart and one soul and they held all their goods in common."[38]

The monks also took from the apostolic model the ideal of renunciation and of penance. Like the apostles, who abandoned everything at the word of Jesus, a monk should abandon everything. (And, notes a monastic author, he should give all that he renounces to the poor, not to his parents; a fitting rebuke to those monastic vocations which had no

[38]Mansi, *Sac. Conc. nova et ampl. collectio,* XX, col. 934. Cf. XVI, q. 1, c. *ex auct.*

other purpose than to prevent excessive division of the family heritage.) They took the notion of obedience[39] from the obedience of the apostles ("Lo, we have left everything and followed you"); likewise penance[40] and even fasting. This is somewhat surprising. Does not the monastic tradition on this point lack precise support in the life of the apostles? It is true that St. James, according to Hegesippus,[41] fasted intensely, that St. Paul spoke of his numerous fastings, that Jesus himself had foreseen the time after his death as a time when the apostles would fast. To these texts the monks added a number of traditions more or less apocryphal.[42] Specifically following Eusebius, who took Philo for the dragoman of the Therapeutae, the certitude became general that the primitive Church gave itself over to fasts so harsh that it was not unusual for early Christians to fast two or three days, even for five days out of six.

Is it necessary to add certain characteristics of dress?[43] The bare feet prescribed for the apostles by Jesus in the words of St. Matthew were respected by certain monks at least in the Orient. Modest

[39]See Hugh of Rouen, *Dial.*, Bk. VI, chap. 4, *PL* 192: 1219B.
[40]See Leclercq, p. 99.
[41]See Eusebius, *Hist. Eccl.*, Bk. II, chap. 23, 4.
[42]See Leclercq, p. 100.
[43]See *ibid.*, pp. 100, 101.

garb was demanded by St. Paul, the narrow-cut tunic in place of the flowing robes of the Romans, a likeness to the appearance of the faithful servant proposed by Jesus as a model to the apostles; this servant, his loins girt, was always ready to be immediately of service to his master. Even in the least details the monks took pleasure in thinking that they observed the rule of the apostles and could legitimately give to their monastic clothing the name of "apostolic habit."[44]

Much more important was the manual work. St. Paul was not the only apostolic proof of this in the eyes of the monks. Were not many of the apostles fishermen, and did they not return to their nets after the Resurrection? It is easy to understand the point in the Rule of St. Benedict: "Then only are they truly monks, when they live by the work of their hands, as did our fathers and the apostles."[45] The Rule of St. Isidore also affirms this in declaring: "All the apostles gave themselves over to corporal work."[46]

Finally the monks felt that they participated, according to the response given by Jesus to the "profession" of the apostles, in the "apostolic hope."

[44] *Ibid.*, p. 101.
[45] *Rule*, chap. 48. On the manual work of the monks, see Siegwart, pp. 242-44.
[46] *Regula monachorum*, chap. 5, *PL* 83:873B.

And this hope was twofold. In one sense, it was the hope of building up the Church. Jesus had promised them, in the person of the apostles, that the apostolic life, practiced with generosity, would be a source of grace for the continual growth of the Church. They thus had the certitude that the observance of their rule was a contribution to the word which led to conversions, because it was itself a preaching by example.

And in regard to God their hope was for the hundredfold. Cassian brought his celebrated conversations with the fathers of the desert to an end with a chapter on the hundredfold promised on this earth to those who empty themselves in the search for perfection.[47] Peter of Celles preferred to consider the promise as it is fulfilled in eternity: "What shall I say of those monks who were the apostles? I would compare them to the angelic spirits with this difference that they have served him, who made himself less than the angels, when he was still clothed in our mortal condition. Yet when crowned with glory and honor by his Father, raised above the Powers and the Principalities, he is seated upon the throne of his Majesty; the apostles are themselves seated on twelve thrones judging the twelve tribes of Israel and perhaps even

[47]See Collatio XXIV, 26, *PL* 49:1320C-1328C.

the angels, as St. Paul says (1 Cor. 6:3). This hope lives also among those who dwell in the cloister. Since their observances are the same as those of the apostles, they have received from Jesus Christ the same promise as have the apostles."[48]

On this point, as on the others, the monks found in the imitation of the apostles a complete guide for their lives. It is understandable that, in the midst of the twelfth century, a Benedictine chronicler, after having recopied the significant verses of the Acts of the Apostles and joining one to the other, was able to write full of enthusiasm: "What element in the sum total of our monastic observances is lacking when compared to the way of life of which we have just written? In this account can be found the hearing of the Word of God, holy communion, prayer, the living of the communal life. Here also is found contempt for riches and the distribution of material things according to the needs of each, the assiduous application to the divine office as well as to almsgiving, the common table, spiritual joy and simplicity. We also express without ceasing the divine praises and thanksgiving; we also are a congregation one in spirit and tranquil, detached from domestic affairs. In a word, all that is discovered in the rules of the fathers, all that is practiced in

[48]*De disciplina claustrali,* chap. 2, *PL* 202:1102D.

the customs of the monasteries, the whole complex is as clear as day in the Acts of the Apostles."[49]

It was not in vain that the monks pondered in their hearts and in their heads what the Sacred Books in no little detail allowed them to learn of the life of the apostles. The history of monasticism, with its remarkable renewals, is to a great extent the fruit of these meditations, a blessed fruit of the Gospel of the apostles. However, these meditations, taken up again, were apt to give rise to quite different results.

[49]"Casus Monasterii Petrishusensis," chap. 11, in *Die Chronik des Klosters Petershausen,* ed. by Feger (Lindau-Constance, 1956), p. 26. The texts cited from the Acts were: 2:44-47; 4:32,34 f.; 5:13.

2

The Canons

1. HISTORY AS URBAN II SAW IT

On January 28, 1092, a little less than seven centuries after Cassian explained how the apostolic life of the infant Church, abandoned by the average Christian and even by clerics, was preserved in monastic communities, Pope Urban II put in writing his own conception of the history of the life of perfection in the Church.

He wrote to a community of reformed canons: "We give thanks to God that you have resolved to renew among yourselves the admirable life of the holy fathers of the Church. Holy Church from its beginning instituted two ways of life for its children. One way indulges those who are weak; the other is designed to lead the happier life of the strong to perfection. The one way leads to the Segor of the little ones, the other to the summit of the mountain.[1] The one atones for daily faults by tears

[1]Gn. 19:17-23. Yahweh, having decided to destroy Sodom, commanded Lot to flee to the mountain. Lot, being fearful, sought and was granted permission to remain on the plain in the little village of Segor.

and almsgiving; the other by ardent and daily prayers acquires eternal merits. Those who live by the first way, the lesser way, make use of the goods of the earth; those who take the second way, the higher way, despise worldly goods and renounce them. But those who by divine favor abandon the things of the world are in their turn divided into two groups the religious purpose of which is almost identical, that of the canons and that of the monks. The latter way of life greatly aided by the divine mercy flourishes in the entire universe; the former, on the contrary, as the fervor of the faithful grows cool, has declined almost everywhere. Yet this is the way of life which was instituted by Pope Urban the Martyr, which Augustine organized by his rules, which Jerome molded by his letters, which Gregory [the Great] commissioned Augustine, the Bishop of the English, to institute. Thus who can think that there is any less merit in reviving this primitive life of the Church under the inspiration and the enduring impulse of the Spirit of the Lord than to preserve in vigor by perseverance in the same Holy Spirit the observance of the monks."[2]

[2]Letter to the church of Rottenbuch in Bavaria, January 28, 1092, *PL* 151:338BD. This passage reproduces it would seem an earlier Bull directed to St. Rufus. See Dereine, "L'élaboration du statut canonique des chanoines réguliers, spécialement sous Urbain II," *Rev. d'hist. eccl.*, 46 (1951), 546. On the importance of the text, *ibid.*, 547, n. 1.

This historical account is important because of its success. Urban II and his successors reproduced it many times, in the years which followed, in their letters to canons engaged in the work of reform.[3] Finally, taken out of its context, this passage was circulated by itself as a precious document in the dossier of the reform of canons.[4] Furthermore the documents which it mentions, namely, the supposed constitutions of Pope Urban I,[5] the rules and sermons of St. Augustine on the customs of the clergy,[6] the epistles of St. Jerome,[7] the letter of Gregory the Great to St. Augustine of Canterbury,[8] all are equally part of the dossier of reformed clerks. Gathered together by Anselm of Lucca in the seventh book of his canonical collection, they were circulated by Yves of Chartres, Peter de Honestis, Liethert of St. Rufus, and Gerhoh of Reichersberg. These docu-

[3]St. Paul of Narbonne, St. Quentin of Beauvais, Maguelonne. His successors utilized it for Mende, Prémontré, Berchtesgaden. Dereine, *op. cit.* (note 2 above), 549.

[4]*PL* 151:535D-536D. See Dereine, *op. cit.* (note 2 above), 546, n. 2.

[5]False Pseudo-Isidorian, *PL* 130:137B-140D. It should be noted that the letter not only recalls the permanence of the common life among good Christians and especially among clerics from the beginning, it also mentions an institution which it attributes to Urban I, the vow of poverty, 140A. Whence the term *instituit* used by Urban II.

[6]*Sermones* 355 and 356, *PL* 39:1568-1581.

[7]See the letters to Heliodorus, *PL* 22:347-355; to Nepotianus, *PL* 22:527-540; to Rusticus, *PL* 22:1072-1085.

[8]*PL* 77:1184B. On the problems raised by this text and the authenticity of the responses of Gregory, see Siegwart, p. 31, n. 1.

ments form a kind of program for the common life of the clergy and are still found grouped together in the Gratian decretals.[9]

Of course this account, like similar ones in the Middle Ages, such as the account of Cassian, is not immune from attack. But this does not mean it is unimportant. Good clerics kept it constantly in mind: it expressed their idea of what the way of perfection in the Church should be and of the place they accorded to it or at least ought to accord to it. Like all historical myth, true or false, it had considerable effect on later events. Moreover it is particularly interesting to us since it claims to discover in the institution of the canons a direct creation of the primitive apostolic Church. This idea has already been considered as applied to monks. What validity does it have applied to canons? This question cannot be easily answered. To answer it at all it is necessary to examine, from the viewpoint of the theme of the imitation of the apostles, the origin of the canonical life and its various renewals in the high middle ages even to the revisions of the eleventh and twelfth centuries.

2. THE ORIGIN OF CANONS IS NOT APOSTOLIC

The origin of canons even more than that of monks is a cloudy part of history. It took place during centuries veiled in obscurity, and it is poorly document-

[9]Q. 1. Ed. of E. Friedberg (1875), I, pp. 676-86.

ed. Only during the last thirty years or so have good historians begun again to interest themselves in it. At the present stage of research this is what seems to be the case.[10]

The name "canon" appears in the sixth century, about 535. It became common in the seventh century during which *clerici canonici* were mentioned. At that time it seems that the word did not designate, as was later believed, clerics faithful to the canons ("canonicals"); rather it designated those clerics who were inscribed on the "canons" or on the list of the clerics of a particular church. These two senses of the term, however, are not mutually exclusive. In fact it seems that one could define canons, as they were in the beginning, in a way that includes both senses. Such a definition would read: Canons are clerics specially conformed to the laws of the Church and particularly bound to their bishop, around whom they are grouped.

At that time the personnel which gathered around the bishop and participated in the liturgy of the various oratories and of the cathedral was numerous and of considerable variety. There were groups of priests under the authority of the archpriests; there were deaconries, or the various charitable and administrative services of the diocese, with the arch-

[10]According to Dereine, *Chanoines,* and Siegwart.

deacons; the higher clergy with their *familia,* that is to say the clerics who assisted them; the *schola cantorum* with its *primicerius;* and then the clerics of the lower orders, lectors, exorcists, acolytes; the ascetics who lived about the church and contributed significantly to its liturgical life; the devout; the more or less professional pilgrims; the penitents; finally, the monks properly so called, who were under the control of the bishop. Some elements of this vast personnel, in which monks were mixed with clerics at the end of the sixth and the beginning of the seventh centuries, gathered in community about the cathedrals for motives which were economic as well as liturgical.[11]

About the middle of the eighth century Bishop Chrodegang of Metz accomplished a decisive step in the development of canons. From the hands of the Bishop all the *clerici canonici* received a rule ordered to the liturgical life. This famous Rule of Chrodegang of Metz, the first truly canonical rule, appeared between 751 and 755. The evolution which, under the increasing influence of the Rule of St. Benedict, made the common life among monks a general thing and gave to monasticism a precise form had its parallel among the clerics. The monastic and canonical rules achieved distinct forms,

[11]See Siegwart, pp. 26-31.

and the personnel of the various churches ceased to be mixed. Communities achieved specialization in one category or another.

Thus began the great Carolingian movement. Charlemagne is responsible for the unification of religious institutions in Europe by which, in large part, the Church today still lives. In 816, after the death of the Emperor, Louis the Pious gave concrete form to an idea of his father by publishing a new rule, the *Regula Canonicorum* of Aix-la-Chapelle. He sent around delegates to whom he granted considerable authority to see to it that this rule was observed. In the ninth century numerous chapters, both cathedral and collegiate, came into existence, staffed with true canons given to the ministry and to the divine office. The character of these canonical chapters carried the deep imprint of the rules of Metz and of Aix and indirectly of monasticism. The traditional observances of the cloister were becoming stabilized. Because of the diversity of canonical communities for which it legislated, the rule of Aix imposed neither the radical renunciation of private property nor the religious vow. However, it did serve to substantially promote the full common life and strict obedience.[12]

Thus exemplary clerics appeared in France, in Lorraine, and in Germany. They lived in commu-

[12]See *ibid.*, pp. 66-68, 252.

nity, had a common dormitory, a common refectory like the monks, and within their monastery practiced a life of observance which in certain places, for example at Hildesheim, achieved a degree of austerity which does not fall far short of that of the strictest monks.

Read for example this description from the *Fundatio Ecclesiae Hildensemensis.*[13] "In the convent (it was after 852 at Hildesheim) the clergy consecrated themselves to the service of God in a manner so religious in its severity and so severe in its religion that the canonical state attained to the rigor of the monastic state. It goes without saying that anyone was subject to harsh reprimand who, I do not say missed, but even arrived late at choir or the table or the dormitory, unless he was excused by some inevitable necessity or by some permission granted. Those inclined to evade the yoke of scholarly discipline found in the cloister tight reins to bind them. They were required to submit for the approval of the dean their daily work of writing or memorizing the Gospel with its homily or the chant or the psalms. Thus the discipline of the cloister was stricter in this regard than that of the school. The brethren did not concern themselves with fine clothes or the pleasures of the table to

[13]*Mon. Germ. hist.*, SS. XXX, pp. 944-45.

which today's clergy are so devoted; they did not decorate their flesh and drape themselves with fine fabrics, but rather clothed themselves in coarse and somber material; finally they were not less familiar with the garb of the cloister than with their traveling clothes. Thus they preferred a rustic simplicity to worldly delicacies; they curtailed their dreams of human successes and looked to nothing as of greater importance than the living of the cloistered life. Enclosed exteriorly as well as interiorly in cloistered severity, they ignored the world without having denied it."

This last trait marked the precise characteristic of the canon.[14] The Carolingian canon did not solemnly swear to abandon the world; he lived and functioned in the world. Because he was a cleric, he was able to exercise a ministry to the faithful. At the same time he lived in a monastery. Here was one of the great periods of collegiate and cathedral canons in the Germanic empire. It was still flourishing under Pope Urban II.

At the conclusion of this historical résumé we are in a position to assess the historical error of Pope Urban. This must be done more explicitly than was required for the historical theory of Cas-

[14]It was at Trier and at Aix that from 966 the canons achieved clear awareness of their specific character as distinct from monks; see Siegwart, p. 252.

sian. The institution of canons does not stem from the church of Jerusalem; it does not stem from the ancient Church. It is quite false to say that the canonical ideal directly flows from the life of the apostolic community. Even if it is regarded as a development of part of the clergy itself, it cannot be associated with the apostolic community. With few exceptions, clerics in the ancient Church lived a private life.[15]

The truth of the matter is that the canons—the *clerici canonici*—were created by a collection of dispositions elaborated by the Church down through the centuries for its clerics to provide for their needs and to further its ideal. Regulations of the ecumenical councils and of the regional synods, customs of the various churches, capitularies, and rules of the Carolingian period are the expressions of these dispositions. They were inspired, furthermore, by biblical texts concerning the Levites, by texts drawn from the pastoral epistles of St. Paul, and by numerous patristic texts.

This dossier does not contain the fundamental texts from the Acts of the Apostles, nor, with one exception of which we will speak later, the moving

[15]See Dereine, *Chanoines,* cols. 355 f.; Bardy, Le Bras, *et al., Prêtres d'hier et d'aujourd'hui* (Paris, 1954), pp. 53-61.

descriptions of the *vita apostolica* to be found in the pages of the fathers of the Church. Verification of this is to be found, for example, in the vast florilegium of biblical and patristic texts which precedes the rule of Aix-la-Chapelle.[16] Also, when this florilegium assembles a number of evangelical texts in Chapter CXIV to demonstrate that the monks are not alone in living the evangelical life, it begins by putting aside the apostolic call: "Go sell what you have, and you will have your treasure in heaven, and then follow me!" This is the explanation provided: "But this precept, and others analogous to it, belongs to the monks alone. They are entirely particular to them, and their importance to them is the greater because they apply uniquely to them."[17]

Practically speaking, by Carolingian times the canons had arrived gradually at a community life. This was not, however, so much a return to the primitive Church as an attempt to imitate, to a greater or lesser degree, the rigor of monastic life

[16]See *Monumenta Germaniae historica,* Concilia II, 1, pp. 307-95. Two sermons of St. Augustine will soon be spoken of. The texts of Julianus Pomarus, Bk. II, chaps. 9, 12, cited in chapters 35 and 108, pp. 356, 383, which urge clerics to renounce their personal goods, rest their position on the example of holy bishops.

[17]*Ibid.,* p. 395 and chap. 115 (the first of the rules properly so called), p. 397, which expressly authorizes the canons to conserve their goods as well as those of the Church.

without accepting poverty in its fullness.[18] The description of the common life of the canons of Hildesheim is characteristic. No reference is made to the life of the apostles. But clearly manifest is the purpose of achieving the level of the monk. Of course in doing this the canons imitate de facto the apostolic life which the monk practiced. Thus they were then indirectly influenced at this time by the apostolic life.

In the time of Pepin the Short, when a powerful movement of reform in the Frankish church was inaugurated by St. Boniface, there was an occasional attempt to stir up the memory of the example of the Church of the apostles. It is not by chance that the rule of St. Chrodegang—a chosen collaborator of St. Boniface—is the first document in the Church to prescribe a feast for each of the apostles.[19] Moreover, when the rule enters for the first time upon the very delicate subject of the obligation resting upon canons to abandon their personal wealth to the community, keeping for themselves only the usufruct, it is by a long and pressing description of

[18]For the Rule of Chrodegang, see E. Morhain, "Origine et histoire de la *regula canonicorum* de S. Chrodegang," in *Miscellanea Pio Paschini* (Rome, 1948), I, p. 175. For that of Aix, *cf.* chap. 115: "Non a cavendis vitiis et amplectantibus virtutibus [canonicorum] a monachorum distare debet vita."

[19]See chap. 30.

the uninimity and of the poverty of the primitive Christians of Jerusalem that the rule exhorts the canons to at least a restricted imitation of this life.[20] Three-quarters of a century later it is manifest that the memory of the early Church haunts more than ever the reformers of the Carolingian period.

This was a time when cloisters and churches displayed great resourcefulness in attributing their origins to some immediate disciple of Christ or of the apostles;[21] when Jonas of Orleans, spokesman it seems of the bishops gathered in a synod of Paris (829), sketched in Chapter XI of his *De institutione Regia* (XX of his *De institutione laicali*), for the use of Louis the Pious and his nobles, an enthusiastic picture of the primitive *vita apostolica*;[22] when the Prologue to the canonical rule of Aix, which retained neither the apostolic description nor the prescriptions concerning property found in the rule of Chrodegang, cites extensively—a unique but significant exception—the two sermons in which St. Augustine explains to the faithful the common life of

[20]See chap. 31.

[21]See J. Zeiller, "Les légendes apostoliques [of France]," in V. Carrière, *Introd. aux études d'hist. eccl. locale* (Paris, 1936), III, pp. 31-40.

[22]See E. Delaruelle, "En relisant le *De institutione regia* de Jonas d'Orléans," in *Mèlanges Halphen* (Paris, 1951), pp. 185-92.

his clerics, directly inspired by the text of the Acts of the Apostles.[23]

This time the apostolic Christian of Jerusalem is no longer invoked as a general example of the Christian, but as the specific model of the diocesan priest, of the canon. Doubtless the two sermons, drowned in a mass of patristic texts and their efficaciousness attenuated by the usages well established in the ninth century which oppose the semi-private life of the canon to the complete renunciation of the monk as well as of the primitive Christian, could have not have had any more effect on the Carolingian canons than the example of Augustine had had until then in the Church as a whole—that is to say, very little.[24]

Nevertheless these sermons are there as something to chew on. They recall that, at the end of the fourth century the Bishop of Hippo, ardently attached from the day of his conversion to the common apostolic life, determined to impose on all his clerics the life of a monastery according to the example of the apostles, and he succeeded in doing so. Was it not likely that these seeds, helped by the considerable authority of Augustine, should one

[23]Chaps. 112, 113 of Aix, *Mon. Germ. hist.*, Concilia, II, 1, pp. 385-95.

[24]See Dereine, *Chanoines*, cols. 356 f.; Siegwart, pp. 16-23, 22, n. 5, on the community life of St. Augustine. Cf. Mandonnet-Vicaire, II, pp. 103-19.

day flower? There is ample evidence that they did from the middle of the ninth century.

Between 845 and 857 in the Province of Rheims the author, or the authors, of the "false decretals" composed to support their ecclesiastical ideas deliberately forged letters of primitive popes of which portions would pass into the canonical collections of the eleventh and twelfth centuries. The following is a passage from them: "Clement, Bishop [of Rome], to the brethren and dearly beloved disciples who dwell with James [the Minor] our very dear brother and colleague in the episcopate [at Jerusalem]. The common life is indispensable to all, dear brothers, and especially to those who wish to serve God without reproach and who wish to imitate the life of the apostles and their disciples."[25] The text of Acts follows: "The multitude of believers, etc."

The letter is not clear as to whether it addresses itself to clerics or to monks; doubtless it is meant for both. But the following letter is very clear: "Urban, Pope, to all Catholics. You are not ignorant of the fact, indeed you know very well, that the common life has flourished not far from all good Christians, and that, by the grace of God, this is the case today. Especially among those who have been set aside for the service of the Lord, especially

[25]*Decretales Pseudo-Isidorianae*, ed. P. Hinschius (Leipzig, 1863), p. 65.

clerics as we are able to read in the Acts of the Apostles: 'The multitude of believers had only one heart and one soul and called not anything their own, that it should be able to be held in common among them . . . .' Whoever then assumes your common life and vows to have nothing of his own should wish in no way to break his promise."[26]

In the midst of the tenth century this form of the apostolic life, enhanced by a powerful eremitical appeal, flourished at Metz where, according to Sigebert of Gembloux,[27] it directly inspired the monastic reform of Gorze which was decisive for Germany. In 975, in the cathedral of Rheims, it influenced the foundation of the "first chapter of regular canons properly so called,"[28] entirely permeated by the ideas of St. Augustine and by images of the primitive Church. In this way there developed in France, in Lorraine, and in Germany the historical aspect of the canonical life which would appear from 1092 in the bulls of Pope Urban II. One can understand the firmness of the Pope's conviction in his error if one remembers the items which the collection of Anselm of Lucques, the great ca-

[26]*Ibid.*, pp. 143, 145.

[27]See "Gesta Abbatum Gemblacensium," in *Mon. Germ. hist.*, Scriptores, VIII, p. 511.

[28]Siegwart, p. 251. Cf., Dereine, *Vie commune*, p. 366, n. 1.

nonical collection of the Gregorian reform,[29] transmitted to him. That text contains: 1) and 2) the false impressions of Urban and of Clement; 3) and 4) the two authentic sermons of St. Augustine on the apostolic life of his clerics, of which we have just spoken; 5) the letter of St. Gregory to St. Augustine of Canterbury on the apostolic life which the missionaries to England ought to live. As for the last, the text ignores that they were monks as well as clerics.

It is understandable also that, taking count of the complete community life of certain reformed canons of the time, Urban II was so categoric in seeing the source of the ideal of the life of the canons in the apostolic church of Jerusalem. This error led to the commission of a grave injustice, since it represents as seriously decadent the common life, which was often quite edifying, of the canons of the Rule of Aix between the ninth and the eleventh centuries. Such is the customary gratitude of periods when the ideal is undergoing a renewal.

3. APOSTOLIC RENEWAL OF THE CANONS

Between the ninth and the eleventh centuries the ideas so artfully insinuated by the authors of the

[29] *Collectio canonum*, ed. F. Thaner (Innsbrück, 1906), I, pp. 362-64.

false decretals slowly gained currency in the Church of the West. For its part the canonical life underwent various changes in the different regions of Europe.

In the Germanic empire, under the powerful hand of the emperors, the great Carolingian colleges of canons, despite ups and downs which cannot be gone into here, preserved vividly the reforming inspiration of Aix-la-Chapelle. They even transformed it, infusing into it the theme of the return to the apostles. At the beginning of the eleventh century, thanks to Henry II, they knew a renewal of splendor in what has been called the Reform of Bamberg.[30] The canons claimed to combine the learning of the church of Liége and the austerity of that of Hildesheim.[31] Some marginal regions, such as the north of Gaul and Catalonia, shared in this stability of the classical canonical life.

However, in France, and still more in Italy, the destruction of the Carolingian influence, the decadence of clerical institutions, and especially the humiliation of the See of Peter, are reflected in the canonical life. The sad condition of the Holy See had led to the descent of Henry III into Italy, the deposition of three popes, the opening of a

[30]See Siegwart, pp. 151-156.

[31]See "Fundatio eccl. Hildensemensis," in *Mon. Germ. hist.*, Scriptores, XXX, II, col. 945.

series of Germanic popes among whom was the great St. Leo IX (1049-1054), and the foreshadowings of the Gregorian reform.

The early ideas of Church reform are those which showed themselves fruitful in Germany. The reforms were aimed first at the head, the pope with the bishops and the clergy, and dealt with their morals generally, with the preservation of their celibacy and faithfulness to their ministry. Moreover the fine canonical institutions of community life which were in the process of expanding in Lorraine and in Germany began to influence the canonical chapters of the Midi.

However, in Italy the reformers lacked the leverage which they possessed in the lands of the empire. There, the reform was the work of powerful seculars, especially the emperor assisted by the greater feudal lords. In Italy this power was too feeble, too far distant, too temporary to function well. Even more, because of its intermittent disappearances, it became even dangerous. For the most part, the temporal power in Italy took the form of local feudal lords or highly ambitious petty princes, who, far from helping the reform of the Church, were directly responsible for its decadence. As a compensating consequence, however, clerics in Italy better preserved a sense of dependence on their bishops and of the primacy of their clerical mission.[32]

How did reform take place? By the most evangelical means possible, the conviction of Christians; and since it is a question of the reform of the clergy, by the conviction of clerics themselves. It was not so much a question of generalizing about institutions supported by the temporal power as it was of bringing about the rediscovery and the return to the true spirit of their lives by the clergy themselves. Thus, by a movement proceeding from the depths of their own conviction and from their own good will, they would rebuild and transfigure the Church.

This explains why in the community-oriented reform movement of the German chapters one runs across very little concerning the *vita apostolica,*[33] and why the ambiguous formulas of the rule of Aix-la-Chapelle are carefully preserved in regard to matters of private property and of community obligations. What inspired the renewal of the Italian clerics and later of others as well is precisely the apostolic life, the return to the primitive Church, the call to "renew the tender beginnings of the Church," to accept in its fullness "the institutions

[32]See Siegwart, pp. 252 f.

[33]Some elements, however, see Siegwart, pp. 164 f., 249-52, and Ch. Dereine, "La *vita apostolica* dans l'ordre canonial du IXe siècle," *Revue Mabillon,* 51 (1961), 47-53.

which the Church had known from its earliest years,"[34] which, above all, included the total renunciation of personal property. The renewal was rooted in an appeal to the primitive Church in all of its purity and in the pristine strength with which it came forth from the hands of Jesus Christ and from the inspiration of the Holy Spirit—an idea always moving to the hearts of Christians and especially to the hearts of priests.[35]

At the synod of Rome in May, 1059, under Pope Nicolas II, the Subdeacon of the Roman church, Hildebrand, the future Pope Gregory VII, in support of the ideal of the apostolic life of the clergy delivered a violent criticism of the canonical rule of Aix-la-Chapelle, condemning it in particular as not sufficiently austere and for allowing canons to retain certain rights to personal property.[36] Though the majority did not go along with his radical attack on private property, he was successful in obtaining a law which encouraged all clerics to adopt the common life at least in those things which are es-

[34]Other contemporaneous expressions: *Ordo ecclesiae sub apostolis; Apostolicae vitae normae; Apostolica vivendi forma; Vita primitivae ecclesiae; Vita nascentis ecclesiae; Formula apostolica; Schola primitivae ecclesiae; Perfectio quam apostoli observare studuerunt; Tenera lactantis ecclesiae infantia; Primordia ecclesiae; Sanctiones Patrum.*

[35]Cf., G. Miccoli, "Ecclesiae primitivae forma," *Studi Medievali,* I (1960), 470-98.

[36]See Werminghoff, in *Neues Archiv.,* 27 (1902), 669. Cf. Mandonnet-Vicaire, II, p. 168.

sential to the apostolic ideal. "We decree, and we require of all clerics in sacred orders who, obedient to our Predecessor have preserved chastity, to have, as is proper for religious clerics, their refectory and their common dormitory very near to the church for which they have been consecrated, and to possess in common everything which they have received from the church. In encouraging these things we demand of them that they strive with all their strength to achieve an apostolic common life,[37] so that having achieved perfection they may deserve to be inscribed in their heavenly homeland together with all of those who receive the promised hundredfold."

We recognize the allusion to the "profession" of St. Peter and to the promise of the hundredfold, the response of Jesus to the profession of the apostles. It is not astonishing that very soon the reformed Gregorian canons began to take a vow after the manner of monks.[38] However, only with the adoption of the Rule of St. Augustine—which is a further question—was emphasis to be placed in the

[37]O. Hannemann, *Die Kanonikerregeln Chrodegangs von Metz u. der Aachener Synode von 816 u. das Verhältnis Gregors VII* (Greifswald, 1914), p. 66, has demonstrated that the accepted text of the canon of 1059 (Mansi 19: 873C, 898B, 908B), "ut ad apostolicam, scilicet communem, vitam pervenire studeant," is faulty. It should read, "apostolicam, secundum communionem, vitam."

[38]See Siegwart, p. 254; cf. pp. 149, 155 f.

canonical profession on total renunciation of personal property.

However, Italian preachers, of which St. Peter Damian is the type, hammered directly at the clergy to convince them to adopt the reform, taking advantage, as a century earlier, of the good will which had stirred up in many a nostalgia for the flight to the desert. Peter Damian, former teacher, then hermit, then monk, founder of the convent of Fonte Avellana, and the most remarkable preacher of his times, in his sermons as well as in his polemical and spiritual tracts constantly and in various ways makes a moving appeal to the clergy. He asks for a return to the original clerical ideal, that of the primitive Church, and exhorts them to rediscover in its fullness the poverty of the apostles which alone will permit them to fulfill as they should their Christian ministry.

These words were soon to be reflected in the gigantic conflict which would convulse the West under the mighty efforts of the popes to bring the reform to fruition. Preaching was not enough to restore the clergy to its primitive ideal. Society had changed its ways. The legal structure had developed in such a way that often spiritual forces were paralyzed; such contrary institutions would have to be broken down at the same time spiritual renewal was being stimulated. This is why several popes, beginning with Nicolas II and especially Gregory VII, did not hesitate to go much further than the preaching of a spiritual idea. By decisions in the legislative and governmental order they struggled to break the juridical bonds which often submitted the clergy to the dispositions of laymen, especially the lay power of determining nomination to positions of jurisdiction. Thus, to achieve the reform of the clergy, Gregory VII was compelled to undertake the investiture struggle, which for fifty years convulsed the entire West. It developed into another struggle which would remain for centuries, that between the priesthood and the empire. From then on Italy and Germany were in turmoil. Everywhere men were forced to take a stand for or against the pope. Europe was shaken by the echo of great battles. The people were called to take a position not only by the combatants or by the polemicists but even by their religious leaders, by the popes themselves. Often, the faithful in their parishes were expected to revolt against their own pastor if he did not submit to regulations issued by Rome.

This attitude of the Gregorian reform is clearly more than a bold effort for renewals; in many ways it can be called nothing less than revolutionary. It certainly took on the appearance of a revolution to the German emperors who until then had been the sincere servants of reform according to imperial law, the accepted law of Western Christendom. They denied that the ideal of the reform was founded on tradition and considered the Gregorian ecclesiastical law as an innovation. They judged especially that the policy of appealing to the people against legitimate authority, whether it was a question of pastors, of bishops, or of emperors (since the popes now deposed emperors themselves), was intolerable and could only destroy the order of the world. However, the stakes were so high—a complete reformation of the clergy—and the need was so evident, at least in the dioceses most immediately under the eyes of the Holy See, that the popes thrust on. The bewildering disorder which was to dominate Church-Empire relations until the fundamental transformation of the German-Roman Empire in the fourteenth century, spread in a remarkable way the ideal of the apostolic reform.

Thus the idea of a return to the sources, of the imitation of the apostles, of conformity to the ministry and to the poverty of the apostles, achieved the distinction that it needed; and the reform of the canons and of the clerics which is firmly joined to it did not remain confined to the southern lands. The new ideal of the apostolic life affected first northern and central Italy and the Midi of France; soon it affected imperial Germany itself, where it sharply modified the earlier reform of many chapters; it penetrated the north of France, the north of Spain, England, Portugal, Ireland, Scandinavia, Poland. New institutions multiplied; profound transformations took place in the clerical system itself. In the beginning the Gregorian reformers intended to reach all clerics. They did not succeed, however, in transforming the conditions of life of the priests in the country parishes, especially those which were still held by laymen. But they did bring about a sharp distinction between the status of canons and that of isolated clerics who would in the future be called seculars. They succeeded only partly, however, in their effort to extend to all canons the ideal of the Augustinian apostolic life. Soon it would become necessary to recognize a new distinction between canons regular and secular canons. Among the latter were unjustly included the canons of the Carolingian or imperial rule.[39]

Finally, among the canons regular themselves considerable differences became manifest. While some collegiate chapters or cathedral chapters took a rule of their own and formed independent houses, at the same time vast orders of canons were constituted, grouping under a general chapter a great number of foundations: the Order of St. Rufus, which re-

[39]See *ibid.*, p. 257.

formed many chapters and colleges in the Midi of France and the north of Spain; the Order of St. Victor, which enjoyed a considerable role in the theological movement; the Order of Premontre, which is today still flourishing; the Orders of Arrouaise, of Springiersbach, of the Lateran, etc.

The psychological side of the history of this powerful movement provides part of its explanation. A troubled conscience was developed in some of the clergy, especially those of the cathedrals and of the collegiate churches. This had much to do with the widespread determination to embrace as fully as the monks the life of the early Church and to bind themselves to it by vow.

While the canons of the ninth century understood from the testimony of the Carolingian rule of Aix that the monks alone were held to imitate the apostles in the total renunciation of material goods, their successors in the eleventh century let themselves be persuaded, in the words of the Gregorian preacher, Peter Damian, "that it is indeed clear and evident that the rule of the canons is modeled on the norms of the life of the apostles, and that any canonical community which keeps its discipline with exactitude imitates the tender infancy of the Church still at the breast. But understand fully the common attitude, the rule of life which the Church observed under the influence of the apostles at the time when the faith was new, 'the multitude had only one heart and one soul and no one called anything his own for everything was common among them. . . .' What then! Should the prerogative [of having property] be accorded to clerics when Christ did not permit it to his apostles?"[40]

There is hardly need to say that at the end of the eleventh century the conflict between the apostolic Gregorian canons and the canons of the Carolingian or imperial type still went on in the colleges of canons,[41] and for the same reasons that in the preceding century there was conflict between Cluny and Gorze and in the following century there would be conflict between Cîteaux and Cluny. It was not a battle of good against evil, but of an ideal which was without doubt superior but was based on a distortion of history, against an earlier and in no way illegitimate ideal.

4. ORIENTATIONS PROPER TO CANONS

A most interesting aspect of this whole question is the manner in which the canons, in accepting fully the inspiration of the apostolic life, formerly the exclusive property of the monks, reacted to this ideal itself.

[40]Peter Damian, *Contra clericos regulares proprietarios,* Opusculum XIV, *PL* 145:486A, 487A.
[41]See Siegwart, pp. 255, n. 2, 256 f.

To measure their reaction in all its fullness it is necessary to concentrate on the moment in which the regular life blossomed among the Gregorian canons thanks to the renaissance of the Rule of St. Augustine.[42] This leads to a complex history into which we do not intend to probe, particularly the involved question of the form in two documents of the Augustinian rule, of the vicissitudes of the first of these texts, the *ordo monasterii,* and of the two canonical observances which sometimes resulted from them, the *ordo antiquus* and the *ordo novus* or *arctior consuetudo.* It was in 1067 that the Rule of St. Augustine was restored at Rheims. At once the example of the apostolic community of St. Augustine, isolated in the course of the history of the clergy, although it had been well regarded during the middle ages, was restored to the first rank and contributed to strengthening the certitude of the apostolic origin of the canonical order.

The entirely reliable form of the Rule of St. Augustine, which as written for women is listed as Letter 211, from the end of the eleventh century

[42]Our first treatment of this problem (Mandonnet, *St. Dominic and His Work,* pp. 121-62), since 1938 has been widely discussed, corrected, and completed. The latest precisions are to be found in Siegwart, pp. 258-61. If Letter 211 and the *ordo monasterii* are not authentic, the rule in the masculine form would be authentic.

circulated one of the most pure expressions of the ideal of unanimity, the central inspiration of the apostolic common life. It begins with these words: "In the first place, [very dear brothers], you should wish to live in your house in unanimity, having only one heart and one soul in God, since it is for this that you have come together."[43]

The Prologue of the Customs of Prémontré, later taken over by the Preaching Friars, comments upon this expression in remarkable terms: "Since the rule lays down that we should have only one heart and one soul in the Lord it is proper that living under this same rule, bound by the vows of the same profession, we should find ourselves equally unanimous in observing our canonical rule, so that the unity which we ought to preserve in our hearts should be vivified and represented to others by the uniformity of our customs. But it is perfectly clear that to be able to practice this observance and to keep it always in mind most fittingly and in its totality, what ought to be done should be written down. Thus each one can learn from the testimony of a text the manner in which he ought to live, and no one will be able of his own volition to change, to add, or to diminish that which should be done. For it is necessary that we be wary, lest by neglecting

[43]Ed. by De Bruyne, *Revue Bénédictine*, 42 (1930), 320.

the least detail we should progress toward decadence."[44]

It seems that no monastic text expresses better than this canonical text the fundamental inspiration of the cenobitic life, namely, unanimous fraternal charity and its direct derivation from the apostolic ideal of Jerusalem ("the multitude of believers had only one heart and one soul"). None better expresses the beneficent necessity of the importance to the Church and indeed to all men of a visible uniformity ("vivified and represented to those outside"). None is more clear concerning the role of observances and of a written text of the rule. The canonical Rule of St. Augustine enunciates with classical clarity the fundamental condition, namely, complete renunciation of personal property: "Call nothing your own that you may hold all things in common, and that your superior should distribute to each clothing and the daily necessities of life, and not equally to each, for you do not all have the same need, but according to the requirements of each one. Thus you are able to read in the Acts of the Apostles that everything was common among them and that distribution was made to each according to his needs. . . ."[45]

[44]Ed. by Martène, *De antiquis ecclesiae ritibus* (Antwerp, 1737, in folio), III, p. 323.
[45]De Bruyne, *op. cit.*, p. 320.

Even more remarkable, however, is the fact that, at the hands of the Gregorian canons the apostolic life underwent a series of transformations, or better, of realignments according to the monastic interpretation. Note for example with what insistence, very significant of the feudal epoch, Peter Damian emphasized the freedom which poverty achieves: "The possession of personal riches results in clerics scorning the authority of their proper prelate . . . and bowing their necks before laymen in the shame and the opprobrium of a ghastly homage."[46] This is a clear reflection of the investiture conflict.

Here a point that is quite novel is raised: the presentation of the regular common life and of the poverty of the apostles as a direct preparation for the ministry to souls. Acts, says Peter Damian, recalls soon after the description of the fraternal and unselfish life of the primitive community of Jerusalem that the apostles, "with great power gave their testimony to the resurrection of the Lord Jesus, and great grace was upon them all" (Acts 4:33). Was this not to make it clearly evident that "they alone are apt for the office of preaching who do not possess the advantages of any worldly riches and who, because they have nothing in particular of their own, possess everything in common"?[47]

[46]Opusculum XXIV, *PL* 145:487D.
[47]*Ibid., PL* 145:488B, 490AB.

The ministry of souls, which was not generally undertaken by monks, became in this way one of the essential themes of the apostolic life. A new document now appears in the history of clerical poverty, set alongside the text from the Acts, namely, the evangelical text concerning the mission of the apostles: "When he sent them to preach, as St. Mark tells us, 'He charged them to take nothing for their journey except a staff; no bread, no bag, no money in their belts (Mk. 6:8).' This is because those alone are apt to the office of preaching who possess nothing of their own. . . . Like light troops (*expediti*), freed from all obstacles, they do battle for the Lord against vices and evil spirits, armed only with their virtues and with the sword of the Holy Spirit."[48]

The apostolic ideal is thus clearly recalled to the ministry. Once again the new orientation results from the needs of the times. The Gregorian movement, which was an effort to reform the Church by the reform of the clergy, was at the same time the inception of a reformation designed to encompass the whole of Christian society, an effort of great magnitude. Putting an end to the equation between perfection and the flight from the world, it sought on the contrary to situate this Christian perfection, especially for the clergy, in a return to

[48]*Ibid.*, *PL* 145:490BC.

the world for the purpose of conquering it in order to Christianize it. During the Merovingian period and even at the beginning of the Carolingian period sanctity could hardly be conceived except for those who departed from the normal life of men. The Gregorian movement very explicitly sought to call all Christians to the life of sanctity while holding their proper places in a Christianity at the summit of which would be the clergy, charged under the papacy with conducting all men, laymen as well as clerics, those who remain in the world as well as those who retired to the convents, to the fullness of the kingdom of God. This courageous and original movement affected Christianity, and even in the West, by making clear that holiness did not belong only to a small elite which consecrated itself to the life of perfection by fleeing from the world, but that it belongs to all those, whatever their work may be, who bear the name of Christian and live well the role in society that belongs to them. This evolution, proper to the Gregorian ideal, reacted on the ideal of the *vita apostolica* which was no longer ordered only to developing virtue in the clergy and to freeing them from temporal ambitions by poverty, but at the same time to preparing them for their ministry in Christianity, as formerly it had prepared the apostles for their ministry of evangelization.

From this time henceforth the apostolic life of the canons is more clearly than ever distinguished from that of the monks. This fact is brought out by a controversy which divided monks, clerics, and canons on the subject of their places in the hierarchy of perfection. It was a curious quarrel both because of its duration and its bitterness, from which there remain to us dozens of tracts, dialogues, and exchanges of correspondence.[49] It had motives more profound than one would at first think, particularly the assurance of the stability of religious and communities in the canonical order by setting aside the exception of the law which permitted a religious to leave his own order for a higher one. Historically, it seems that, for the canons, it amounted on the one hand to the correction of the thousand-year-old interpretation given by the monks to the theme of the imitation of the apostles, and, on the other, to the elimination of the very recent interpretation of the secular clerics. Finally, it poses the decisive question, namely, in what does the true imitation of the apostles consist? Does it mean the common life with its observances, or the ministry to souls, or does it include both at the same time? The source of the dispute is to be found in the changed condition of the monks. Formerly laymen,

[49]A list is to be found in the article of Dereine cited in n. 2 above, 558 f.

by the beginning of the twelfth century monks were very often clerics. In this way they are similar to the canons. At the same time they practiced more perfectly than the canons the rule of life of the apostles. Were they not then the true successors of these same apostles?

There was also another factor to be taken into consideration. By an ancient tradition, all conventuals, whether monks or canons regular, were excluded from every kind of ministry. It was for this reason that the secular clerics opposed both to monks and to canons regular the phrase of St. Jerome that "the office of the monk is not to instruct others but to lament."[50] Or again the words of Rupert of Deutz: "If you proclaim yourself a monk, you proclaim that you are dead; for one is not a monk if he is not dead to the world. But how can one be dead if he causes his voice to be publicly heard?"[51]

However, monks and canons argued against the secular clerics by insisting that their fundamental conformity to the apostles did not consist in the fact that they preached, baptized, or exercised any sort of ministry. The activity of the apostles was much more than these ministries! They performed

[50]*Contra Vigilantium Liber, PL* 23:367A. Cf. above, chap. 1, n. 31.

[51]*Altercatio monachi et clerici, quod liceat monacho praedicare, PL* 170:537C.

miracles, they produced great fruits of grace by their preaching, they achieved conversions and baptisms en masse. But the seculars do nothing like this. They should stop saying, then, that they imitate the lives of the apostles by their activity. The only possible way of imitating the apostles is to practice their virtues. It is precisely that which the monks and canons regular do. Monks and canons, if they are priests, have, therefore, much more than the seculars the right to the ministry of the apostles and to pre-eminence in the apostolic life. If that were not the case, remarks one of these opuscules, "it would be necessary to say that the most impure of clerics, because he preached and baptized, practiced the apostolic life."[52] To understand the word "impure," it is necessary to remember the charges at that time against secular clerics for violation of the rule of celibacy.

There remains the opposition between the monks and the canons regular. The canons insisted that they were clerics well before the monks, that they went back at least to Levi! If the monks were clerics it was only by way of exception, only that they might fulfill some office in their monasteries. The canons regular then shared more than the monks in the ministry of the apostles. Thus the canonical

[52]*De vita vere apostolica,* Bk. II, chap. 15, *PL* 170:631D-632B.

customs of St. Rufus were able to conclude: "The incontrovertible verdict of the fathers of the Church decides solemnly that the order of canons should be by every right placed above all others. This is not astonishing, since it carries on the work of Christ and the apostles in preaching, baptizing, and administering the other sacraments of the Church."[53]

It is apparent that, despite the efforts of Pope Urban II in his résumé of history to derive symmetrically from the apostolic tree the canonical and monastic orders as two branches of equal dignity, the canons of the Gregorian reform, because they were clerics by definition and possessed a proper ministry, considered themselves closer to the apostles than the monks, since they were equal to them in the rigor and the poverty of their community life.

At the conclusion of the canonical development of the theme of the imitation of the apostles it already appears why a century and a half later the same spiritual theme would emerge concerning the apostolic orders devoted to preaching, whose members came to be called mendicants.

[53]*Coutumier du XIe siècle de l'ordre de S. Ruf*, ed. A. Carrier de Belleuse (Sherbrooke, 1950), p. 97. It is an opinion already defended in 1091 in a celebrated letter of Ivo of Chartres; see Dereine, *op. cit.*, (n. 2 above), 544 f. Pope Urban II did not entirely follow this opinion when he placed the monastic life and the canonical life on the same level.

3

The Mendicants

1. THE NEW SIGNIFICANCE OF THE WORD "APOSTOLIC"

In the course of the thirteenth century the words *apostolic, vir apostolicus, vita apostolica, regula apostolica,* took on a new sense which was different from the earlier meanings. Up to the ninth century or even to the tenth the adjective "apostolic," when it was applied to a way of religious life, was strictly *monastic.* In the eleventh and twelfth centuries it came to signify the religious life of the *canons* as well. In the thirteenth century it no longer belonged solely to the one or to the other. When an inhabitant of Albi, for example, declared before the Inquisition that the "Perfect" Catharists are of the *regula apostolorum,*[1] he had no intention of saying that they were either monks or canons. The three terms: monastic, canonical, apostolic were opposed to one another, and, what is more curious, there was not only a distinction but also a gradation.

[1]See. C. Douais, "Les manuscrits du château de Merville," in *Annales du Midi* (1890), p. 185.

The liturgical office of St. Dominic, composed before 1242, declares in an antiphon: *Tandem virum canonicum auget in apostolicum.*[2] *Auget!* It was not simply that he replaced the one with the other, but it was a question of rising from the canonical ideal to the apostolic ideal (*vir apostolicus*).

James of Voragine, in his *Life of St. Dominic,* composed between 1271 and 1288, put it this way in a paragraph where he played on the word, *Dominicus=a Domino custoditus*: "The Lord truly watched over him in the three states of his life; the first of which was the state of a layman, the second that of a canon regular, the third of an apostolic man (*vir apostolicus*). In the first he watched over him in helping him to begin well, in the second to progress well, in the third to achieve perfection."[3]

Note again the *crescendo*: a layman, a canon regular, an apostolic man. And again, *incipere=proficere=perfectionem apprehendere,* which corresponds to the three degrees of religious perfection according to the Eastern tradition. As total a difference is found then between the canonical and the apostolic as between the lay and the canonical.

Somewhere around 1278 Stephen of Salagnac, indicating three steps in the religious practice of

[2]Dominican Breviary, first antiphon of the second nocturn, Aug. 4.

[3]*Legenda aurea,* ed. Graesse (Dresden, 1846), p. 466.

St. Dominic, comes up with the same *crescendo*: "He was a canon by his profession, a monk by the austerity of his regular life . . . to which he added as a result of growth in grace, the elements of the rule of the apostles."[4]

This time Stephen of Salagnac dots his i's and makes very precise the elements he ascribes to this *regula apostolica.* It is nothing like what is indicated during the first millenium (a common life with renunciation of property), nor in the eleventh and twelfth centuries (the rule of St. Augustine). It is now: "Do not travel by horse; push through the various countries to evangelize and to work for the salvation of your neighbor; carry with you neither gold nor silver, and be content to beg for your food."[5] A little earlier an anonymous preacher expressed himself in analogous although somewhat less detailed terms: "The apostolic life consists in leaving everything to follow Christ and to preach him and to serve him in poverty."[6] St. Thomas himself said: "The apostolic life consists in this—that having abandoned everything they should go throughout the world announcing and preaching

[4]"De quatuor in quibus . . .," ed. Kaeppeli, in *Monumenta O.P. Hist.*, 22 (1949), pp. 8-9.
[5]*Loc. cit.*
[6]"Tractatus de approbatione ordinis Fr. Praed.," ed. Kaeppeli, in *Arch. Fr. Praed.*, 6 (1936), p. 145.

the Gospel, as is made plain in Matthew 10:7-10."[7]

Some fifty years earlier, in 1211 to be exact, a Cistercian, Peter of Vaux-de-Cernay, already expressed in terminology quite similar to that of Stephen of Salagnac the formula of the apostolic life: "To do and to preach (*facere et docere*), according to the example of the good Master, presenting oneself in humility, going on foot without gold or silver; in short to imitate in every way the life of the apostles."[8]

It is evident that the theme of the imitation of the apostles, pondered upon by the men of the new age, in the new European climate, raised new ideas and new institutions different from the familiar ones of the past. This was the moment for the appearance of the apostolic or mendicant order of which the four great ones exist today, namely, the Preachers, the Minors, the Carmelites, and the Augustinians. They are the fruit of these new ideas.

We will limit ourselves to examining the origins of the Order of St. Dominic or of the Preachers to which all of the texts cited pertain. Certainly it would have been possible to build the same study about the Order of St. Francis. But the history of

[7]*Contra impugnantes Dei cultum et religionem,* ed. Mandonnet (Paris, 1947), p. 47.

[8]*Historia Albigensis,* ed. P. Guébin and E. Lyon (Paris, 1926), I, n. 21.

the Preachers more completely and more clearly exemplifies the movement with which this essay is concerned. It is not by accident that it is the first of the mendicant orders. The basic idea of the mendicant orders is clearly delineated from its creation in 1215, and by 1220 it had developed in a matter of five years to the point where its direction was sufficiently set so that its founder, St. Dominic, was able to die in the following year without fear that it could not yet live on its own. It was to rapidly develop without deviating from its initial direction.

2. DISCOVERY OF APOSTOLIC MOBILITY

St. Dominic had known for a long time and by experience the ideal of the imitation of the apostles according to the interpretation of this notion still flourishing among the canons regular.[9] The chapter of the cathedral of Osma, into which Dominic entered between 1196 and 1197, had been in existence for only a half century and still flourished in the fervor of its foundation as a chapter under the Rule of St. Augustine. It had as its head a good bishop, Martin Basan, and a holy prior who would soon become bishop, Diego de Acedo. Two years later the superiors of the chapter obtained from the

[9]See Vicaire, *St. Dominic* (henceforth designated: *St.D.*), pp. 36-39, 41-42.

pope a bull which definitively protected the chapter against the lay appointees whom the King of Castile had for some years imposed upon it and which permitted the revival of the full common life according to the pure inspiration of the rule.

Until 1215 Dominic kept his title of Canon of Osma, remaining faithful throughout his life to the essential elements of the life of canons regular, namely, intense contemplative prayer joined to the official liturgical prayer of the Church, a yearning for the community life, and a taste for unanimity or harmony of spirit among the brethren. But in 1206 at the very latest, and very probably much earlier, in Spain, or at least during his three years of traveling in Europe, he came to know a new possibility of developing the imitation of the apostles.[10] In May or June of 1206, at the famous meeting of Montpellier between the legates sent by the pope against the Albigensians and the Bishop of Osma whom he accompanied, Dominic gave himself permanently to this new ideal. The scene has been reported by many contemporaries. No account is as important as that of the Cistercian, Pierre des Vaux-de-Cernay.

This account dates from 1211, hardly five years after the events. It is the work of the secretary of

[10]See *ibid.*, 49-53, 72-76.

the principal person involved in this meeting, the Abbot of Cîteaux, legate of the Apostolic See; and this secretary is known for his minute material exactitude. Moreover, since it antidates the foundation of the Preachers and is the work of a Cistercian, there is no reason for its author to improperly exaggerate the importance of the events which it recounts as the prelude to the entire *Historia Albigensis.* Here is the account: "But it happened when he [the Bishop of Osma] returned from the curia and came to Montpellier that he found there the venerable Arnaud, Abbot of Cîteaux, Brother Peter of Castelnau and Brother Raoul, Cistercian Monks, legates of the Apostolic See. In their discouragement they wished to give up the legation which had been imposed upon them, since they had gained nothing or almost nothing by their preaching among the heretics. Each time they sought to preach to them the objection was raised of the evil conduct of the clergy. But if they wished to do anything about correcting the life of the clergy, they would have to interrupt their preaching.

"In this apparent impasse the bishop offered them some wise counsel. He admonished them and counselled them to work with more ardor than ever at their preaching, giving up every other care. But to close the mouths of the malicious it would be necessary to *do* as well as to preach [Acts 1:1] according to the example of the good Master, to show themselves to be humble, to go about on foot without gold and without silver [Mt. 10:9], in short to imitate in every way the life of the apostles. The legates, however, did not wish to adopt on their own authority these ways of acting which were innovations. They declared that, if anyone properly authorized would undertake to precede them in behaving in this manner, they would very willingly follow him. What more need be said? This godly man offered himself."[11]

It is known that this decision of the bishop launched Dominic on the work of preaching in the Midi of France. It also gave his preaching its special inspiration and, nine years later, it inspired the institution of his Order. "And that was the cause of the institution of the Order," declared the early friars.[12]

One phrase of the legates thrust to the heart of the matter, sketching in detailed precision the kind of life that, with the bishop and the legates, Dominic would assume for the future. "Each time that they sought to preach to the heretics the objection raised was of the evil life and conduct of the clergy!"

[11] *Historia Albigensis,* I, n. 21.

[12] Etienne de Bourbon, *Anecdotes historiques,* etc., extracts by A. Lecoy de la Marche (Paris, 1877), n. 83; cf. n. 251.

It has been concluded a priori from this phrase that the clergy of the Midi of France were thoroughly lax and that the legates had not fulfilled their mission of correcting the clergy. As if it would have been enough for the Catholic clergy to have been good clerics, obedient to the canons, chaste, disinterested, zealous, to prevent the heretics from finding their conduct unworthy! The Albigensians were not Catholic, but Catharists and Vaudois. To reform the clergy according to their ideal it would have been necessary to transform them into Vaudois preachers or into the "Perfect" of the Catharists. For, in effect, both assumed the position in principle that only Christians who live expressly after the manner of the apostles have the right to preach the doctrine of the apostles. Others, whether pope or simple pastor, had not the right to call themselves ministers of the Lord. Moreover, the imitation of the apostles was understood by the Albigensians quite otherwise than it was understood by the monks and the canons. From the New Testament it is possible to sketch many ways of imitating the apostles!

We have seen that, among the monks from the end of the fourth century, those of Syria and of St. Chrysostom had a way of understanding the apostolic life that adapted it very well for missionary evangelization. For even better reason there was a similar interpretation of it by certain clerics and bishops. This interpretation was carried to extremes by certain fanatics whose one-sidedness eventually resulted in their separation from Catholic unity and orthodoxy. When monasticism came into being, certain "apostolics" or "apotactics," catalogued later by St. Epiphanius, seemed to have conceived as the apostolic ideal a singularly disturbed preaching activity.[13] Later the Messalians, the Paulicians, the Bogomils of Bulgaria or of Bosnia, and eventually in the twelfth century in the West the different kinds of evangelical preachers raised up by the heretic Lombards and Albigensians followed an analogous line. All the apostolics of this tradition, however, were not dissidents. Some itinerant preachers of France, from the beginning of the twelfth century to the Poor Catholics of the first decade of the thirteenth century, a series of good Catholics, manifested the possibilty of living within the Church itself an apostolic ideal entirely different from that of the monks.[14]

The imitation of the apostles of which Diego spoke at Montpellier refers expressly to this ideal, the imitation of the itinerant life which the Twelve lived under the guidance of the Lord. The description of it is found in the Gospel, among other places

[13]See Spaetling, pp. 3-35; Siegwart, p. 236.
[14]See Spaetling, pp. 43-47.

in the account of the mission which Jesus confided to the Seventy-two, truly a practical exercise of preaching. "[He] sent them on ahead of him, two-by-two, into every town and place where he himself was about to come" (Lk. 10:1-16, cf. 9:1-6; Mt. 10:5-16; Mk. 6:7-13), and gave them on this occasion the very concrete counsel from which it is possible to draw a complete program of life. These are the essential elements:

1. A personal mission, that is to say a vocation and a mandate. Each of the apostle-preachers heard the "come follow me." Each had received a mandate: he was sent, *missus*. The point is very important; it is precisely the *mission* which the heretics did not possess.
2. A ministry, an *officium*, conferred by the mandate: the preaching of the Gospel. "The kingdom of God is at hand; repent, and believe in the gospel (Mk. 1:15)."
3. At the same time a precise and exacting way of life: total poverty. It is no longer a question of divesting oneself of one's own goods to live henceforth without personal property but from the goods of the community; poverty is to be absolute. There is to be no property at all, neither individual nor common: "Have neither gold nor silver nor money in your belts"; do not even carry bread with you;

do not have either a bag or a wallet for your journey. For daily subsistence one must depend on good will, on daily charity; "have no care for tomorrow." Nourishment depends upon the discretion of those one meets along the way and especially upon those to whom one preaches. It is necessary to accept what is offered; there are no forbidden foods. This is an important precision which departs from the practice of the monks in this matter. One should eat what one is offered and as it is offered, lest one give pain or embarrassment to the host. Nor should one pass from one host to another. Clothing also ought to be poor, limited to one tunic. Finally the feet should be bare; St. Mark, however, allows the use of sandals. Likewise, while Luke and Matthew say that the preacher should not have even a staff, St. Mark permits one. He is then a little less austere than the other two. Here is a slight scriptural problem which in times when inspiration was understood in a fashion too material gave occasion for disputes on the Gospel.

Such then is the first part of the picture of the apostolic life; it can be summed up in two words: mendicant poverty.

4. Another element is mobility; it is necessary to travel. What a difference from the life of the Cenacle! Do not wait for men to come, but go into the city and into the villages wherever the Lord ought to be. That is to say, into the entire universe. One must go without rest, go swiftly; "Do not greet anyone on the way" (a neat Eastern touch which graphically signifies the haste of the trip). But when a destination is reached a greeting is given. However this "peace" which one gives upon arriving, if by chance those to whom it is offered are not worthy of it, returns to its author: a little apostolic economy. Finally shake the dust from your feet if anyone does not receive you, that you may owe him nothing. Thus is created the spirituality of the road. *Vos estis hospites et advenae,* you are guests and pilgrims. You are not to be settlers. From this is drawn the spirituality of the *peregrinatio pro Christo,* of becoming an exile for Christ. It was that which in the seventh century set those doughty Irishmen on the road under the guidance of St. Colombanus and caused them to cover a good part of the West, renewing Western monasticism.
5. Finally the last element, which must not be neglected. In this traveling there is an affinity

for the common life. It is not the solitude of St. Paul. Two-by-two should they go. Certainly the community is not large, but it is already sufficient to permit charity, as the Fathers of the Church who comment on this text observe, for it is sufficient that there be two in order that fraternal charity may be practiced. It is by design that manual labor is not added to these elements. It is not that one never encounters it among the apostolics who devoted themselves to evangelization. It was a tradition too unanimous in the whole history of the movement of perfection. Canons regular of the *arctior consuetudo,* for example, had considered themselves obliged to work with their hands by the *ordo monasterii* and still more by the example of St. Paul. This was true at the turn of the thirteenth century of the Humiliati of Lombardy and of the first companions of St. Francis. However, other apostolic groups, such as the Vaudois and the Catharists, clearly rejected it: work, as the Scripture says, for "the food which endures to eternal life" (Jn. 6:27). It would be a crime, they thought, for one who was consecrated to the work of the Gospel to work with his hands lest he would give part of his resources to something other than spiritual

> work. So strong was the conviction of these evangelists on this point that it separated them from the worker-apostles by an irreparable division.[15]

Such is the program of the apostolic-evangelical life, so different from the apostolic life of the Cenacle, which from 1206 Dominic adopted for his own. He lived it for nine years in Languedoc, then in Spain, in France, and in Italy. In 1214 he extended it to the group of preachers who little by little grouped themselves around him. Finally, in 1215, he decided to make it the formative idea of his Order. In this, an apparently insoluble problem is encountered: it even seemed somewhat like squaring the circle.

3. THE ITINERANT IDEAL STABILIZED IN AN ORDER

Down through the history of the Church there had been numerous itinerant evangelical preachers similar to Dominic as far as his personal ministry is concerned. At the turn of the thirteenth century a certain Fulk of Neuilly in the environs of Paris offers a remarkable example.

A special difficulty of practicing this life in the Church had become particularly prominent during

[15]See G. Gonnet, "Waldensia," *Rev. d'hist. et de philos. religieuses,* 33 (1953), pp. 219, 223 f., 230.

the half century before the time of Dominic. This evangelical way of life had fallen into bad repute because it had become almost the monopoly of clerics in revolt against the Church (e.g., Arnaud of Brescia, Henry the Monk of Lausanne), or of participants in schismatic movements such as that of the Vaudois, or even violent heretical and anti-Catholic movements such as the Catharists. The reaction of the Church had already become general and was concretized a few months after the foundation of the Preachers in Constitution 13 of the Lateran Council (1215). There is clear evidence that, in forbidding the establishment of new religious communities, or of untried ways of serving God, the Council was particularly concerned with the new mode of the apostolic preaching life.[16]

But that was not the principal obstacle. What had, until the thirteenth century, always prevented the establishment in a religious society of the itinerant imitation of the apostles and had made every attempt at such an establishment for a century and a half run aground was something that seemed an irresolvable conflict. It appeared evident that the wandering initiative of the apostolic preacher was incompatible with community life. It seemed impossible to reconcile personal mendicancy with the life of an institutionalized, stable convent.

[16]See *St.D.*, p. 340.

The problem consisted in this, that in wishing to devote oneself to constant preaching, in delivering oneself to the spirituality of the road, it would be necessary to plan, if one wished to form a permanent fraternal body, for a home base for the preachers. It would be necessary for the preachers to have a place of rest, a place where they could be provided for in sickness or old age, and especially a place for instruction, for reflection, for work. Dominic, less than anyone else, would be willing to neglect sacred study.

Furthermore, it would be necessary to form novices in virtue and learning; it would be necessary to provide them with the spirit of their state of life and to teach them to pray and to work. How could this stability be provided without a convent, without an organic community? The apostolics that Dominic had constantly before his mind, the Vaudois especially, rejected this sort of thing. If one were to accept the idea of a community, a house, possessions, a stable installation, what would become of the spirit of day-to-day poverty? What would become of the complete abandonment to Providence day-by-day? What would become of the complete dependence on the charity of others in any situation? St. Francis, who had also been touched by the spirit of the itinerant apostolic life after his conversion, rejected the idea of such an established base throughout his entire life. He wished a movement in which nothing would be a source of restraint, in which no one would have any kind of possession. The first Franciscans were expected to rely on chance lodgings, in caves for example, and be prepared to leave them if anyone wished to reclaim them. To have nothing and to avoid in any way sinking roots, was this not the logic of the itinerant apostolic life?

But St. Dominic was a cleric. He had the spirit of stability. As an Augustinian canon he recognized that the life of the apostles did not include only mendicant wandering but also the life of the Cenacle, a way of life for which he had full appreciation. Why should one be sacrificed to the other. And indeed the apostolic preaching ideal had, as has already been seen, an affinity for the life of community. It was necessary to go two-by-two. Did this not open a way to a solution?

Moreover, the dissident apostolics themselves, the Catharists, relied upon the support of certain institutions. The wandering "Perfect" accepted hospitality in the communities of the deacons or of the ladies of their sect. The communities of female "Perfects," who preserved the right to possess, provided also bases for the preaching of the "Perfect." St. Dominic had himself tried from 1207 to support his mendicant preaching by a center of this kind at Prouille. There he had gathered some young women who, converted and abandoned by their Catharist families, did not know which way to turn.[17] In this way the first of Dominic's convents was established. These women received or accepted donations, and they sheltered the Preachers between their trips.

By 1215 St. Dominic no longer remained there. At this time he established community life with his brothers.[18] He received at Toulouse a house where he took up residence. This would be the Cenacle where his novices would live, where the students he took to the capitular master of theology (his name has come down to us, Alexander Stavensby) would study, and where the fathers would be able to rest between preaching assignments. In fact the charter of the foundation of the "House of Preaching" of Toulouse, as it was called, foresaw as residing in the house brethren occupied in various ways with preparation, with regaining their strength, with recovering from illness. In order to provide for their necessities, including the purchase of books, the bishop assigned to them part of the tithes of the diocese. At the same time he conferred upon them the mission of preaching everywhere in his diocese.

[17]See *ibid.*, pp. 118 f., 121. A like situation was established at Madrid in 1219-1220; see p. 253.
[18]See *ibid.*, pp. 168-79.

The brothers imitated, then, the apostles in the totality of their life. They imitated the apostles in the house, living in it as in a cenacle. They had a common fraternal life with liturgical prayer (for the apostle who goes out and who preaches is also the one who should render praise and intercede at mass and other public prayer), and with study and repose. Then they would imitate the apostles on the road in announcing the word and confiding themselves each day to Providence. James of Vitry, who would see the first Preachers at Bologna about 1222, would describe them as "canons-preachers."[19] He was quite exact. From 1215, even before Innocent III, to satisfy Constitution 13 of the Lateran Council, which required Dominic to explicitly inscribe his Order in the classical formulas of the canonical tradition, Dominic had joined the itinerant life of the mendicant apostle with the life of the cenacle of the canon regular. With that he seems to have realized the synthesis of the ancient community apostolic ideal and of the new itinerant apostolic ideal.

Yet it is necessary to look closer. The two elements do not fuse easily; their opposition is of considerable proportions. Without raising either of the incidents which in 1217 would manifest the pres-

[19]Vicaire, in Mandonnet, pp. 285-88.

ence of a split,[20] it is enough to note the very different character of the two types of poverty which the Preacher ought successively to practice. On the one hand personal property was renounced but the common goods of the community were available within the convent; on the other hand one lived the life of a beggar while on the road preaching. It is known that in 1215 Dominic had accepted from the bishop as the means of subsistence for his community a sixth part of the tithes of the diocese, that is to say, the part which the canons classically reserved to the poor. The brothers were treated as poor, and that which they received was the donation of the faithful to whom they addressed the word of God. Moreover, the bishop in the charter of foundation multiplied detailed regulations in order to give this regular gift the precarious aspect of an alms. However, the fact remained that this gift was a revenue, it was regular and a fairly dependable resource. What would become, then, of the spirituality of daily abandonment to Providence which at the same time the Vaudois (shortly before converted by St. Dominic)—the Poor Catholics—practiced under his eyes with a quite different splendor?

"We have renounced forever, 'they said in their proposed way of life sanctioned by the pope in

[20]See *St.D.*, pp. 237-38 (revolt of John of Navarre).

1208-1212,' and we have given to the poor whatever we possess according to the counsel of the Lord. And we have decided to be poor in such a way that we would have no kind of care for the morrow and we would accept of no one gold, silver, nor anything of that sort, except clothing and nourishment for each day."[21]

That is why Dominic chose another way.[22] In 1220, after having tried it at Paris and at Bologna and having discussed it at Rome where the pope accepted it, he had "conventual mendicancy" adopted at the first general chapter of the Order. Every day two of the brethren left the convent to beg from door to door, and the convent lived on what was obtained in this way. Thus the convent itself lived in the same spirit as the preacher on the road. It waited each day for what Providence would choose to send it. There have come down to us from the beginnings of the Dominican Order accounts of occurrences growing out of conventual mendicancy. One, for example, was narrated without embellishment by the procurator himself at the process of Dominic's canonization. One day when the convent had nothing to eat this distracted procurator went to tell Dominic that it was useless to

[21]J.B. Pierron, *Die Katholischen Armen* (Freiburg-im-Breisgau, 1911), pp. 173, 176, 179 f.

[22]See *St. D.*, pp. 266, 273 f., 283 f., 310-12.

ring the bell for the meal since there was nothing to put on the table. Dominic told him to gather the brethren together anyway. They went to the table; the blessing was given, and Dominic remained in prayer. Two young men appeared at the door of the refectory, entered and placed before each of the brethren a golden brown loaf of bread which was quite sufficient for their meal. It is the famous episode, the dinner brought by angels, that Fra Angelico so often painted.

There are also stories centering around the humble mendicancy of Dominic himself. One morning in Dugliolo, a little village of northern Italy, he was going from door to door seeking alms. A man gave him a whole loaf of bread. Dominic went down on his knees to receive it.[23] At this time he was a man well known throughout the Church. He was a friend of Pope Honorius III, of Cardinal Ugolino, and of many other prelates. He had been sent on this mission by the pope for the renewal of the north of Italy, a mission as important in the eyes of the papacy as that in which he had but recently participated against the Albigensians. This religious founder, this great servant of God, went

[23]See "Processus canonisationis Bononiensis," ed. A. Walz, in *Mon. O.P. Hist.*, 16 (1935), 42. An English translation will be found in F. Lehner, *Saint Dominic: Biographical Documents* (Washington, 1964), p. 130.

down on his knees because a peasant gave him an entire loaf of bread.

Such is the spirit of the legislation which in May, 1220, five years after its foundation, Dominic caused to be inscribed in the first constitutions of the Preachers in four simple words: *possessiones et redditus nullatenus recipiantur* (neither property nor revenues of any sort should be accepted). There is no question of manual labor. Dominic had settled that like the Albigensians. What then remained for their subsistence other than the precarious alms of the faithful? The mendicant orders had been founded. What this means is that orders of firmly-established communities now abandoned themselves, just as traveling preachers, to daily Providence. Dominic was indeed right to give to his brothers, to vivify their exercises and to inspire their attitudes, an exemplary image of the true evangelical preacher of which the constitutions of 1220 contain such a remarkable standard.

This passage from the first constitutions of the Dominican Order gives the flavor of this crucial instant at which the two parts of the life of the apostles met and were joined. It describes the moment when, renewed, instructed, armed with the energies and qualifications acquired in the religious community, the preacher went forth to fulfill the mission confided to him by the Church: "The Brothers who are capable of it when they go forth from the convent to preach should receive from the prior a companion for the road, a companion the prior considers suitable to their character and dignity. They then receive a blessing. Then they take to the road and behave everywhere as men who seek their own salvation and that of their neighbor. They live in the perfection of the religious spirit. As men of the Gospel they follow the footsteps of their Lord, speaking with God or of God between themselves or with their neighbor, avoiding familiarity with suspect company. In thus going forth to exercise the ministry of preaching or in traveling for any other reason they should not accept nor should they carry with them gold, silver, money, or gifts of any sort except that which is necessary for their nourishment, their clothing, and other objects of necessity and books. None of those who are deputed to the ministry of preaching or of study should receive the charge or administration of temporal affairs, that they may be able more freely to dispose themselves to fulfill well the spiritual ministry confided to them. At least they should have to occupy themselves with these necessities only when no one else is available for this purpose, since there is nothing wrong with assuming a temporary care for the necessities of a particular journey."[24]

4. THE IMITATION OF THE APOSTLES, FORM OF THE APOSTOLIC ORDER

The apparent simplicity of the texts as well as of the foundation ought not to conceal the enormous difficulty involved in achieving the synthesis of so many disparate elements drawn from so many, independent, anachronistic historical traditions. The prehistory of the apostolic orders as well as their later history suffices to make the gravity of the problem clear.

It is difficult to avoid at first glance the impression that the founder of the first mendicant order constituted something of a discordant amalgam, an *ens per accidens,* in superimposing, perhaps as part of his plan for competing with the heretics with whom he was doing battle, the life of a mendicant preacher on that of a contemplative canon. The latter way of life was itself an amalgam of the clerical life and the monastic life. What is one to think, for example, when one reads in the little work of Stephen of Salagnac, which has already been cited, a panegyric of St. Dominic, glorifying him for having gathered the best of Benedict, of Augustine, and

[24]Primitive Constitutions, Part II, chap. 31, in Lehner, *ibid.*, pp. 246-47.

of the rule of the apostles and even adding luster to all of that?[25]

This is especially true if one considers that Dominic, in order to surmount the difficulties which this situation presented, had to produce two laws which seemed to strike at the very solidity of his institution itself. The first of these laws was the provision for dispensation which gave to the superior the power of freeing a religious, if he judged it necessary, to further his work of study or of the salvation of souls. The second was the declaration made after his death, but expressly willed by him, that the rule should not oblige under guilt of sin but only under the penalty of the penance.[26]

It is easy to see that there would be continual conflict from the very beginning, varying according to circumstances both physical and psychological, of the often antithetical elements gathered together in the lives of mendicant religious. It is true that conflict was not inevitable, since it must be remembered that under certain aspects these elements had some affinity for and complemented one another.

But the true answers to these doubts about the profound essential unity of the type achieved in the thirteenth century by the mendicant orders, espe-

[25]See note 4 above.
[26]See *St.D.*, pp. 303-5.

cially by the Order of Preachers, is to be found elsewhere. If one returns to the origin and to the different steps of the foundation of St. Dominic it is possible without too much difficulty to throw light on the cause, in the strict sense of the term, of this essential unity. The creative element in the psychology of the founder was ceaseless meditation on the evangelical theme of the imitation of the apostles. It was a tenacious will to more perfectly achieve the integrity of this ideal. Pope Gregory IX, when someone spoke to him of the canonization of his friend, Dominic, said: "In him I have known a man who realized in its fullness the rule of the apostles, and I do not doubt that in heaven he will find his association with them."[27]

Yet even as there existed a subjective cause of unity in the inspiration of the founder, there was also an objective form of unity in the purpose which he envisaged. The apostles actually existed, and the diverse activities which the monks, the canons, and the mendicants in succession sought to imitate under the name of the apostolic rule, the Twelve actually synthesized in their personal lives. In meditating upon the Scripture and returning constantly to the words of Jesus to the apostles, the medicant religious had the means of renewing

[27]Jordan of Saxony, "Libellus de principiis O. Pr.," ed. Scheeben, in *Mon. O.P. Hist.,* 16 (1935), n. 125.

without ceasing the inspiration which brought into unity each of the six fundamental elements of their way of life: fraternal unanimity (Acts 4:32), poverty carried to the extent of seeking only day to day needs (Mt. 10:9 f., 6:34), common and public prayer (Acts 2:46, 3:1, 6:4), an intense private prayer (Acts 1:14, 2:42), indefatigable journeying (Mk. 6:6-13), and the evangelical preaching of salvation (Mt. 10:7 f.).

There was no need to abstract nor to ponder for a long time. The great figures of the apostles, sketched at the beginning of these three chapters, were presented easily to their hearts as to their imaginations, recalling them by turn without any incompatibility to each of these elements. It was not a dead text which provided the friars with a synthesis of them all, but it was an example that had been lived, indeed that is living still, the presence of transcendent leaders, whose composite images blend together in that of Jesus Christ the Master, the Savior "whose footsteps they followed as evangelical men."

Thus the only suitable denomination, even the only adequate definition of the orders of mendicant preachers, seems to be that of "apostolic orders." This expression not only has the advantage of manifesting the apostolic principle which sustained them, which had gathered together in the course of centuries the elements of their institution, and especially which provided the essential point of their unity as well as of their vital source in Holy Scripture, namely, the apostolic life.

At the end of this essay it would not have been without value to recall some of the stories from primitive Dominican sources which illustrate the traits of the evangelism of the Preachers which flowed from their imitation of the apostles.[28] It is not only in the simple scenes of abandonment to Providence, or of mendicancy, of charity and unanimity in the common life among the brothers, of generosity in the preaching of the Kingdom and of the peace of God, but also in the accounts of vocation, of profession, or of their last moments upon earth that the reader at each depth can perceive as a fresh and pure note the resonance of the Gospel. The life of the brethren had point and unity only in the imitation of the apostles. And that life in return throws light upon the Gospel.

As this essay comes to its end it seems that, in a special way, it has been possible to measure the fruitfulness of an evangelical theme, the theme of the imitation of the apostles down through the history of the Church. Entire sections of the history

[28]See M.-H. Vicaire, "L'évangélisme des premier fr. Prêcheurs," *La vie spirituelle,* 76 (1947), 264-77.

of the movement of perfection and of the history of the clergy in the Church have in some instances been brought out of the shadow as one traces this long line of light. Before such a historical study it would have been difficult to imagine all the richness of four verses of the Acts of the Apostles and a few from the Gospel on the basis of simply dissecting them philologically, even by meditating upon them. The history of the Church is the most vivid and the richest commentary that one is able to provide on the Gospel. The reality, especially when it is that of an immense cohort of authentic Christians trying to live or to relive the word of God with all generosity, exceeds the imagination of commentators however learned or believing they may be. It is striking that the fruitfulness of some of the interpretations of this theme has not always been in proportion to their authenticity. Errors have not prevented the good effect of certain misunderstandings. The historical error of Cassian regarding the institution of monasticism, the egregious error of Gregorian times concerning the history of the canons regular, even the erroreous idea that the monks, canons, and mendicants had of the primitive Christian life at Jerusalem and of many other things concerning the infant Church did not render their Christian life invalid. The verses of the Acts are extremely brief, the precepts given by Jesus on the occasion of the mission of the apostles are too particular to be universalized without precaution, to be made absolutes, principles. St. Thomas made this point in the thirteenth century.[29]

Moreover, the exegetes have known for a long time that the first Christians did not share all their goods in common; that Christ and the apostles did not practice begging from door to door as a Friar Preacher of the thirteenth century; that they did not go barefoot as the primitive Friar Minor did.[30]

Does this amount to saying that all these religious were mistaken? Does it mean that the apostolic ideal

[29]The precepts which Jesus gave to the apostles, for example, when he sent them to preach, are not applicable to every situation and at all times. They can be interpreted as (1) *concessions*. Jesus allowed the apostles to take nothing with them when they went to preach, to depend upon the faithful for their support. To take with them enough to provide for their needs, as St. Paul did, is not a sin; rather it is a work of supererogation. Or they can be interpreted as (2) temporary regulations, no longer applicable after the Passion, according to Luke 22:35. Whence the conclusion: "Jam imminebat enim tempus perfectae libertatis, ut totaliter suo dimitterentur arbitrio, in his quae secundum se non pertinent ad necessitatem virtutis" (*Summa Theologiae*, Ia IIae, q. 108, a. 2 ad 3). St. Thomas said this to counter the fanaticism of the "apostolics." It is not aimed at the apostolic rule of his own Order, to which he was devotedly attached, as is evident from his life as well as from his polemical works (such as the *Contra Impugnantes*) in defense of the mendicant orders.

[30]As expressed by Thomas of Sutton, O.P.: "To go about without shoes is a good penance, but it has nothing to do with evangelical or apostolic perfection" ("Contra aemulos fr. O. Pr.," in *Arch. Fr. Pr.*, 3 (1933), 77).

which sustained, nourished, and inspired them did not produce in the Church institutions of enduring value? Does it demand of the members of these institutions that they no longer seek in the theme of the imitation of the apostles the principal source of their inspiration? Is it necessary to return to the explanation of the secular clerics at the beginning of the twelfth century in their quarrel with the monks and the canons regular and to say that the only way of imitating the apostles is to preach, to baptize, to offer sacrifice as they did, or, if prelates, to govern the faithful?

It seems that this history clearly gives rise to the conclusion that, throughout its entire existence, the Church has understood that the ministry of the apostles, the apostolate in the highest sense of a term much misunderstood, cannot be practiced in a legitimate Christian and consequently fruitful manner without at the same time trying to practice a certain rule of life. To legitimately continue at any level of apostolic action it is necessary to cling to the attitudes concerning which Christ himself has given counsel and command to his apostles. Some hold to them by their state of life, that is to say, by vow; others by the manner of acts which they perform. But all, secular clerics or religious, must remain faithful, if they wish as their Master and the apostles in the Gospel, *facere et docere* (to do and to teach): to teach that which they practice and to practice that which they teach. The apostolate requires the apostolic life, if one wishes to be a Christian apostle. And this apostolic life is of such great value even for those who have not received the apostolic ministry that it is able to be for them also the school of perfection, that it is indeed the classical school of Christian perfection.

We can say, then, that the monks, the canons, and the apostolic religious, in their ceaseless meditations drawn from the same texts, not only have not been led astray but, in taking account of certain historical and exegetical rectifications, they have essentially attained definitive revelations of the school of perfection as of the ministry of the Lord Jesus Christ.